John Guest is an ordained minister with more than 30 years' exp[...] ministry, and a professional clown. With over a quarter of a century [...] in local primary and secondary schools, he loves telling stories (parti[...] [...]dren) and spends much of his time in the ten schools around his parish. Joh[...] enjoys cooking, travel, languages and creative writing and occasionally admits to playing the piano and accordion. He is Rector of St Margaret's Parish Church, Stanford-le-Hope, in Essex. His first book for Barnabas, *Collective Worship Unwrapped*, was published in 2005.

In loving memory of Joan Doreen Guest, 1923–2005. Mother, you taught me well.

Obey the teaching of your parents—always keep it in mind and never forget it. Their teaching will guide you when you walk, protect you when you sleep, and talk to you when you are awake.

Proverbs 6:20–22

Acknowledgments

My mother died suddenly in her sleep just a few days before my book, *Collective Worship Unwrapped*, was published in 2005. For almost 50 years of my life, she and my father were the constant teachers whose instruction I didn't always follow but whose values and example I will always be grateful for. I am who I am largely because of them: I get my character from my father and my personality from my mother. Thank you both!

Our teachers, the professionals and the 'volunteers', deserve a huge vote of thanks for making us the people we are today. I would like to thank all the staff and children of Stanford Primary, Abbots Hall Primary, Graham James Primary, Arthur Bugler Infants, Arthur Bugler Juniors and St Joseph's for all your encouragement over the past 16 years. In addition I would like to thank Eastwood Middle School, Brookhill Leys Middle School, Tilbury Manor Nursery and Infants and St Katherine's C of E Primary. I would particularly like to thank the staff and pupils of Glebe Primary School and St Mary and St Nicholas Primary School, for assisting my research and for teaching me when I was a pupil with you over 47 years ago.

I can never repay what I owe my family. Ben and Hannah, I am so proud of you both. One of my greatest privileges has been to be your dad. Kim, you are my best friend, you were part of the magnificent seven who climbed Kili with me in 2005 and you have taught me more than anyone else I know. You are the best! I love you! Thank you.

Thanks a million to the church family at St Margaret's, Stanford-le-Hope, to my colleagues, Janice, Rosemary, Rob, Matt, Steve, Janice, Lynn and all the brilliant team in the office, and to all the others who hold my arms up. To Sue Lester and Linda Sheerstone for proofreading and much loving support. To my good friend, Dave Cooke, for setting out the scores for the songs. To 'Big Bob' and to Steve and Ted, all stooges for John Two, and my dear friends Chris and Peter for a dining-room table and a great deal more.

Thank you also to those whose contributions of insightful wisdom have helped make this book what it is: Petra Back, Sue Basnett, Camila Batmanghelidjh, Kathleen Bienvenu, Joan Burnes-Hopkins, Alan Clark, Christine Cooper, Kathryn Copsey, Angela, Philip and Bethan Davies, Aarya Deonarain, Sue Doggett, Steve Duggan, Richard Epps, David Etherton, Nicky Everett, Jackie Feeney, Alice Flett, Gill Gibbons, John Gladwin, Laurie Green, Sandra and Paul Griffiths, Peter Hartley, Denise Helliwell, Ella Hutt, Graham Jiggins, Bente Kumar, Chris and John Leach, Elaine Lyon, Bryan and Val Mann, Linda Moore, Rosemary Morgan, John Peoples, Margaret Redmond, David Richards, Mary Taylor, Anne Walton, Wayne Whiskerd, Moira Wickens, Dot Williams and Margaret Withers.

Finally, to the many teachers whose patience and faith have shone like jewels along the path of my development. I owe you more than you know and I never thanked you enough. And once again, to my parents, both the one on earth and the one in heaven: Ken and Joan. You taught me well.

And for you, Jesus, my teacher and my friend. All my collective worship is unwrapped and offered to you.

Text copyright © John Guest 2010
Illustrations copyright © Simon Smith 2010
The author asserts the moral right
to be identified as the author of this work

Published by
The Bible Reading Fellowship
15 The Chambers, Vineyard
Abingdon OX14 3FE
United Kingdom
Tel: +44 (0)1865 319700
Email: enquiries@brf.org.uk
Website: www.brf.org.uk

ISBN 978 1 84101 664 1

First published 2010
10 9 8 7 6 5 4 3 2 1 0
All rights reserved

Acknowledgments
Scripture quotations are taken from the Contemporary English Version of the Bible published by HarperCollins Publishers, copyright © 1991, 1992, 1995 American Bible Society.

FLAKE, BOOST, DOUBLE DECKER, TIME OUT, STAR BAR, CRUNCHIE, BUTTONS, DAIRY MILK, CURLY WURLY, DREAM, FUSE, FUDGE, ROSES, TWIRL, TWISTED, WISPA, PICNIC, FREDDO and HEROES are trade marks of the Cadbury group of companies, and are used with the kind permission of Cadbury UK Limited.

FERRERO ROCHER is a trade mark of Ferrero Rocher and is used with the kind permission of Ferrero UK Limited.

A catalogue record for this book is available from the British Library

Printed in Singapore by Craft Print International Ltd

More Collective Worship Unwrapped

20 tried and tested story-based assemblies for primary schools

John Guest

Preface

Hello everyone; welcome to our assembly! Welcome to some *More Collective Worship Unwrapped*!

Let me start by telling you a story. Once upon a time… there was a vicar who was very nervous about meeting people and standing up and talking in public. She was especially nervous about standing up and talking to children. She felt really guilty about this because she felt that she ought to talk to people about God and that she ought to go into her local school and talk to the children. The trouble was, she just didn't know where to start. One day she met a teacher who confessed (after a bit of arm-twisting) that actually he was nervous about standing up in front of children, too. And as for taking a school assembly…!

Sounds incredible, doesn't it? A vicar and a teacher who were nervous about public speaking! Now maybe the idea of leading a school assembly doesn't fill you with a sense of dread, but actually there are more of us lacking confidence in this area than you might think. There are very few of us who wouldn't benefit from a bit of timely encouragement and inspiration in this area. I am pleased to tell you that the vicar and the teacher were able to encourage and inspire each other and, before too long, they managed to get hold of some really useful resource material that gave them lots of ideas about how best to proceed. They still made lots of mistakes and they still got quite nervous at times but they both realised that even the longest journey begins with a single step and they had been able to take that together. After a while, their assemblies became famous and other vicars and other teachers (not to mention quite a few other people besides) got involved and began to make a real difference. And do you know what? They both lived happily ever after!

When people like you and me go into local schools to meet classes and lead collective worship, we have the most incredible opportunity to make a difference. A head teacher I know once told me, 'Children are not vessels to be filled, they are lamps to be lit!' Those of us who work with children have the unique privilege of 'lighting lamps' when we form partnerships between schools and the local community. We may feel nervous and ill-equipped but, as we work together, many creative gifts are released to our mutual benefit.

The local trust I lead has the motto 'Building Bridges, Forging Friendships, Lighting Lamps' and this is essentially what we are doing when we meet with children, parents and teachers in our schools. The Balstonia Trust project (Stanford-le-Hope, Thurrock, South Essex) represents not just the convergence of need and opportunity in our schools but also the partnership we are developing between education, community and church. There is more on this and other contacts in the Resources section at the end of this book.

There is a wealth of material currently available for everyone involved in leading collective worship (or 'assemburly' as it is known to most younger children) in schools. However, as in so many areas, what we do is not always as important as how we do it. This book, a follow-up to my previous work, *Collective Worship Unwrapped*, doesn't claim to have all the answers but it should be able to get you started. This book, like its predecessor, sets out in a simple way the areas that need to be our focus when considering school assemblies: the preparation, the environment in which to 'perform' and how to use the material available. I very much hope that you will bring creativity and imagination to these assemblies and thus make them your own.

Enjoy the book and, above all, have fun!

John Guest

Contents

Photocopiable visuals

foreword

In January 2009 I left Stanford-le-Hope, having spent the last seven years of twelve there as head teacher, to take up my new post as head teacher at St Peter's School in Billericay. During my time at St Joseph's I met and worked with many interesting characters, developing strong and lasting friendships. Among these was John Guest, an Anglican priest. Over the years since we first met, John and I have enjoyed sharing assemblies together in an ecumenical way, reflecting on our shared values.

John would come to St Joseph's once every month and deliver one of his assemblies to the children as he would do in many of the state primary schools in the area. The children looked forward to the 'Mr Guest assemblies' very much because he had the gift of being a true storysmith. I used to marvel at the way in which he could captivate the children with familiar Bible stories told with a twist or with a story designed to deliver a strong moral message. I never knew what was going to happen next but I could be safe in the knowledge that the children would have enjoyment while learning. Sometimes John would arrive in character, sometimes he would bring props and sometimes, as a real treat, he would bring his accordion and we would both play a hymn together during the assembly. Sometimes I would just be a passive bystander and other times he would have me involved in the story. Either way, I confess that I looked forward to his visits as much as any of the children, and this was probably true for the majority of the staff. He brought the Gospels to life in his own inimitable manner.

John has kindly collated and recorded his assemblies so that others can share them, too. *Collective Worship Unwrapped* made these wonderful assemblies available for children and assembly takers. The world was introduced to the Toolshed Gang (much loved by the infants at St Joseph's), Honky the Donkey and many others. In this new compilation I am pleased to see some new additions to the Toolshed Gang, as well as the arrival of Mrs Bitsy and her dear friend, Mrs Barjonas.

As a head teacher of a faith school, I am always looking for high-quality assembly resources with a strong Christian message. This book provides exactly that. The stories are told in a fun way that can be enjoyed both by the storyteller and by those listening. I was honoured when John asked me to write this foreword. It was my good fortune to have been associated with him during my time at St Joseph's. I unreservedly commend this book as a valuable resource for the busy teacher or head teacher—a real gem.

John Peoples
Head teacher, St Peter's Catholic Primary School, Billericay

Introduction

This section includes suggestions for getting the most out of collective worship, and is a follow-on to the introduction in *Collective Worship Unwrapped* (Barnabas, 2005). *More Collective Worship Unwrapped* provides a further 20 story-based assembly outlines to be used with Key Stages One and Two. Those familiar with the previous book may be pleased to see some more stories of The Toolshed Gang and The Two Johns, as well as another adaptation of Tolstoy's short stories and a further adventure of Honky the Donkey. There is also a new set of stories for younger children, looking at some of Jesus' parables through the eyes of a motherly teddy bear. Using a toy as a proxy for their own feelings can often help younger children to express themselves. As before, each of the assembly outlines gives a Bible base, tips on presentation, a list of visual aids required, recommended songs, an optional prayer and follow-up material. An idea of the level of preparation required is provided.

GETTING STARTED

When it comes to leading assembly, whether we are experts or 'first-timers', good preparation is vital. Any carpenter, painter or decorator will tell us that half the task is in the preparation. Get the wood, wall or window properly 'prepped' and we save ourselves a lot of grief afterwards. We can usually tell if a job was inadequately prepared by the standard of the finish.

This principle is even more evident when it comes to addressing children and young people in school. Any activity that involves interaction with a group of people needs to be carefully planned. Take conjuring, for example. A good trick will need to be repeated over and over again at home before being tried out in the public arena. For maximum effect, conjurors need to cover every eventuality, so they will practise dozens of times, even to the point where they can carry out the procedure with their eyes closed. The better the preparation, the better the presentation; and the better the presentation, the better the penetration.

Here is a checklist of elements to consider when preparing for collective worship, whether we are using conjuring, puppetry or drama, or just telling a Bible story.

Resources

We need to make sure everything we need is close to hand, such as the matches to light a candle or the projector required to display a colourful acetate. Check that the visual aids are in good condition and carefully organised so that no one gets the idea the assembly has been thrown together a few minutes beforehand. Make sure the visual aids illustrate the topic clearly and are appropriate for the children. In this book and *Collective Worship Unwrapped*, there are suggestions for visual aids to accompany every assembly.

Personal presentation

We need to ensure that we are clean, neat and appropriately dressed. The aim is to do nothing that might put a barrier between ourselves and the children. Personal hygiene and fresh breath are important areas to watch.

Timing

This is very important! 'Better late than never' is the watchword of the sluggard. 'Better never late' is better. Allow plenty of time to check for any potential difficulties, such as not having enough space for children to come out to the front or an extension long enough to reach the projector or CD player. We will also want to ensure that any items we expect the school to provide—such as a screen or a small table—are available. All these details require time, so we need to be sure that we have it. Also, we need to confirm how long the assembly is expected to last. As a rough guide, 15–20 minutes should be allocated, but, if there are lots of younger children present, the time may be even shorter. We need to keep an eye on the clock.

No matter how well we prepare, however, unplanned incidents will occur. Children will always come up with statements that catch us off guard. They often delight in embarrassing us or taking us down an avenue that we didn't expect. Good preparation should ensure that these incidents enhance rather than interrupt the assembly.

EVOKING THE SENSES

The environment in which we deliver an assembly will also be crucial to how well it is received. Creating a calm and peaceful setting in the area where collective worship is carried out is very important, so it is helpful to hold collective worship in surroundings other than where the children usually sit and work. The establishment of the environment will relate very strongly to the senses, and the children will often respond positively to their first impressions as they enter the designated hall or classroom. School halls can often be very adaptable to a positive spiritual atmosphere. If clear guidelines are laid down for acceptable behaviour in collective worship time and if the guidelines are consistently and sensitively underlined, then the 'otherness' of this time and space can be effectively communicated. Since assembly is also an ideal opportunity for teachers to give notices and to administer a 'telling off' where necessary, the 'otherness' aspect may be a little compromised, but this need not be a major problem.

Here, then, are some suggestions for establishing the environment.

What we hear

This should be addressed first, as hearing will be the first sense impacted, even before the children enter. Music should be used most sensitively, as it can powerfully affect mood and attitude and can enhance or destroy the environment right from the start. Some schools are very good at creating the right atmosphere through music, others less so. Some schools have a 'composer of the week' and display the titles of the pieces being played, but lack of musical knowledge or lack of competent musicians is often used as an excuse for little or no musical content to an assembly. Interestingly, where music is used more to set the scene, the children appear more receptive and less inclined to be disruptive.

Music sensitively delivered can enhance the experience of collective worship. Pieces that are calming and relaxing are especially helpful for Key Stage One and Foundation children.

What we see

There is huge scope through the medium of sight: pictures, colours, materials and objects can all convey positive experiences. Lighting will also be an important factor and should be used creatively. Closing drapes and blinds can be effective in establishing a 'holy space' but there also needs to be an element of 'openness'.

Candles and fresh flowers can be very helpful. Lighting a candle is a very evocative act that can involve the children themselves. It can signify a moment of silence, reflection or prayer. Balloons and bubbles can also illustrate reflection or celebration. A media projector can display all kinds of images to enhance the environment as well as to illustrate talks, and is often a good aid to opening and closing the assembly time—children might enter and exit to an appropriate visual display accompanied by suitable music. Visual presentations of children's work, illustrating a project or aspect of the curriculum (pictures, drawings, collage, mobiles, photos and other displays), can improve the appearance of the collective worship space.

What we smell and taste

Smell and taste are perhaps not senses that we usually associate with collective worship. They may not be as important as sound and sight in establishing the environment for collective worship, but their use can still be taken into account. After all, worship in many churches (and some schools) will involve tasting bread and wine, and some churches will use the very distinctive smell of incense.

If we are aware that these senses are at work, we can use them in a positive way. A pleasant or evocative smell in the hall, or an assembly that includes tasting things, is certainly worth considering. For example, an assembly on the prodigal son might involve a large bowl of hummus, possibly with a wooden spoon sticking out of it. We could suggest (not inaccurately) that this is something like what the prodigal son had to eat and invite some of the children to look at, smell or even taste it. Proper hygienic safeguards would be needed, of course, but it is an interesting use of the senses. Let's not underestimate the value of what we taste and smell in collective worship.

What we feel

This sense will be active throughout an act of worship and long after it is over. I am utterly convinced that worship should be an enjoyable experience and, as such, it will involve the 'feel good factor'. Put simply, if the children enjoy the assembly, it will be a good, positive and pleasant experience for them; if they don't, it won't!

There are lots of factors associated with the sense of feeling (some of which we may be unable to control). We should give some thought to how the children come in to assembly, where and how they sit and who they sit with. One of my local schools encourages the children to sit anywhere they like on the floor rather than putting them in rows by class or year grouping. Most primary schools are happy for their pupils to sit on the floor but, however the children are seated, we need to be aware of their personal comfort (or lack of it!) and their attention span. I think 5–20 minutes is about right. In any event, no school assembly should last more than half an hour.

'Awe and wonder' as a concept is difficult to quantify. Sometimes it happens accidentally, but it is more likely to occur if we have prepared carefully, taken proper account of the needs of the children and invited God to participate.

THE ART OF STORYTELLING

The art of storytelling has been around for ages and we are seeing more and more storytellers coming into schools, to the delight of children, parents and staff alike. Storytellers will often spend a whole week in a school, working in different classes, taking assemblies and possibly even offering a public performance of their skill. Lance Pierson, himself a wonderfully accomplished storyteller, says the following in his excellent book *Storytelling* (SU, 1997, p. 5):

I thought of the college lecturer who told me about the latest discovery made by post-modernist communicators. 'It's no good trying to persuade people with reasoned arguments and lectures today,' he said. 'The way to get through to them is with stories.' And I thought, 'Surely the wisdom of the ages (not to mention Jesus, the master storyteller) knew this already.'

Lance's book is a good one to read, not just to discover a wealth of new stories to enjoy but also to help us find the best way to read and tell those stories. A lot of us find it incredibly daunting to think of standing up in front of a room full of people (especially children) to tell a story. Although telling a story is a bit like telling a good joke, we still find it difficult. Many people feel understandably nervous about taking assembly. Even vicars, pastors and other church leaders who are quite comfortable preaching to their congregations become anxious at the idea of communicating with two or three hundred children. Assembly will usually involve telling stories—reading them if we must—and making them vital and interesting. Certain skills are active in this process and many of them can be learnt.

Learning how to speak and to appreciate the value of words will help us greatly in communicating with children. Here are some pointers that might help our storytelling technique.

Knowing the story

Stories can be told or they can be read. If we are attempting the former, we will certainly need to have committed the tale to memory. If we are sufficiently accomplished, we will remember the highlights and use our imagination to fill in the gaps. Reading a story from a book can also have great value—although, if it is a picture book, we will want to find a way for the children to appreciate the artwork. Whether we read or tell, we will always need to prepare carefully. Remember BBC's *Jackanory* ('I'll tell you a story of Jackanory; now my story's begun. I'll tell you another of Jack and his brother; now my story is done')? The readers on that programme were reading from a book (or possibly an autocue) but we just knew that they had spent a lot of time preparing themselves and probably knew the story by heart. In most cases, the better the preparation, the better the story.

Engaging the listener

A good story, well told, will always engage the interest of the listener. Nevertheless, we may want to use a variety of techniques to enhance this engagement—for example, audience participation such as responding to particular words or phrases in the narrative. When telling a story to children, we might want to include comic interludes such as getting things obviously wrong and having the children interrupt with the correct information. This technique is often used in pantomime: 'He's behind you!' ... 'Oh, no he isn't!' ... 'Oh, yes he is!' and so on. Examples may be seen in the assemblies 'Honky the donkey', 'Samson the superhero' and 'Peter the escape artist' in *Collective Worship Unwrapped*.

Narrative repetition

Narrative repetition is a classic technique used in storytelling and appears in many traditional fairy tales—for example, the wicked queen's oft-repeated question of the magic mirror in 'Snow White and the seven dwarves' or the threefold response of the troll in 'The three Billy Goats Gruff'. Sometimes the technique of repetition is used to build suspense in a narrative, so the listeners become more excited as they think, 'We've heard this before; we know what's going to happen!' You'll find this technique a number of times in the Bible: see, for example, the story of the fiery furnace in Daniel 3. There is also an example in the story 'Arthur and the magic fish' in *Collective Worship Unwrapped*.

Simplifying the tale

At Clown Camp they teach the K.I.S.S. principle: 'Keep It Simple, Stupid!' Stories don't need to be overly complicated. The best ones usually have a very straightforward story line and development—for example, the classic fairy tales of Grimm and Anderson, the parables of Jesus and a good number of the other Bible stories. Making stories complicated, with ever more tortuous plots and twists in the narrative, works well in the written and read form, but a story that is told needs to be simple so that it holds the listeners' attention. For example: 'Man goes on a journey, gets mugged and needs help. Three people see him; the least likely helps him.' The moral is made and the story ends. This is a pretty uninteresting précis of the story of the good Samaritan but there are endless ways to tell a simple tale. We just need to keep the basic outline clear-cut. Make it difficult and people soon begin to lose interest.

Spice it up a bit

The much over-used phrase 'Variety is the spice of life' is actually very meaningful when we think about it. Variety saves us from bland mediocrity—a good story can be ruined if it is told too often or always in the same way. Spice can make a meal interesting, even surprising, and can call forth radical reactions from within. Stories can be like that, too, if they are imaginative, creative and varied. I recommend *Tales of Grace* by Eve Lockett (Barnabas, 2005) as a great source of well-spiced stories.

Variety is important not only in the content of the story but also in the way we tell it. If we change the pace of the narrative or the volume, then, like the piquant spice or the surprising chilli pepper that we discover in a meal, the story will jolt the listeners' capacities and deepen their appreciation of the event. Try starting a story with 'Once (pause) upon (pause) a (pause) time (pause) there (pause) was (pause) a (pause)…'. Or, how about 'Once… once upon… once upon a… once upon a time… once upon a time there… once upon a time there was… once upon a time there was a…'. See how variety can be used even in the simple classic start to a story.

Stay focused

The most successful jokes work best when they have a good start and a humorous punch line. What we put in between is up to our own creativity and imagination. Similarly, our stories will need an attention-grabbing start and a punch line that leaves the audience thinking and possibly wanting more. The journey between the beginning and ending may employ any of the techniques listed above, but it must progress consistently and in a disciplined way. Paying attention to detail requires practice and care but it will lead to a high level of excellence in the telling of the tale. Focus in the narrative will also ensure that we retain the interest and approval of the listener.

Smile!

It's surprising how much difference a positive attitude can make. Short or long, biblical or secular, the tale needs to be told with vibrancy, passion and enthusiasm. Then, even the sorriest story will animate our listeners and raise their interest levels significantly. If we show the audience that we enjoy the story, then they will enjoy it too. In collective worship, we need to focus on the child right at the back and be determined to communicate the story to him or her. If we believe in what we are doing and project our enjoyment of the story, we will hold our listeners in the palm of our hand.

When I was younger and tended to embellish my experiences with rather fanciful narrative, adults told me sharply, 'Don't tell stories!' I think they meant 'Don't tell lies' and with that I heartily agree. Stories, on the other hand, are not lies, even though many of them are not factually true. (If stories had to be 'true', we would require Jesus to prove that the good Samaritan, the sower and the prodigal son all existed independently of the parables in which they appeared.) The fictional nature of parables and stories makes them no less valuable to us. They continue to be a vital resource in the communication of education, entertainment and encouragement.

GATHERING RESOURCES

Although stories are at the heart of an assembly, we will need to have access to a great many more resources if we want to make an effective contribution to collective worship. When I first started taking 'assemburly', back in the 1970s, people generally had to make it up as they went along, coming up with their own ideas and trusting in the innate power of the story. Nowadays, I'm glad to say, there is a veritable treasure house of material available to use with various age groups. A great deal of this is accessible through the Internet (see, especially, www.barnabasinschools.org.uk).

Most of the collective worship material that is available in book form has been written for anyone to use. Provided we check the copyright permissions and so on, it is fine just to go ahead and use it. It is well worth taking a stroll around a local Christian bookshop and leafing through some of the material that is on offer in this format. As I just mentioned, the Internet is also a very useful source of collective worship material: as well as Barnabas, many Christian publishers and children's organisations have excellent websites. For Anglicans, the diocesan children's and schools' officers will have much to offer. Try logging on to a local diocesan website for information on the work being done by the education department. In my diocese of Chelmsford, there is a scheme allowing schools to become affiliates for a modest fee, thus enabling them to access many good training and partnership prospects.

It is, of course, important to be creative in the use of other people's material. Anybody can simply rehash someone else's ideas, repeating parrot-fashion what another person has put together. The best value to be gained from using someone else's material is to let it become a springboard for our own thoughts, applied to our own context. The stories and ideas I glean from a variety of books are always better for being adapted to the local scene and the kind of children I am addressing. It is only common courtesy to credit the originator of the idea where that is appropriate, but there is no reason why those same ideas should not encourage our own creative abilities to rise. We need to use our imagination, our own adapted visual aids, our own voice characterisation and so on. Our collective worship will then become as individual and unique as we are.

The best resource of all, without doubt, is the Bible. When I first introduce people to the Bible, I remind them that it is not actually a book but a library. There are 66 books in this library, each of them with its own particular appeal. The Bible is far more than just a story book, history book, poetry book or theology book: it is a huge resource that encompasses all these things and a great deal more.

Each of the assemblies set out in the assembly books I have written includes a Bible link—a passage from the Bible to read before taking the act of collective worship. Sometimes it is good to read the Bible aloud to children or listen to someone else read it, live or recorded. It is also good to encourage children themselves to read a portion of the Bible aloud (with help if needed). Modern translations of the Bible are invaluable and it may also be helpful to look at modern paraphrases. The translation I use throughout my assembly books is the Contemporary English Version (CEV). Once again, the Internet has some good links to Bible sites, such as www.biblegateway.com or www.bible.com. I have found many fascinating pages on these sites and a host of Bible translations in many languages and styles.

The Bible is now available in many formats as well as different translations. Lance Pierson, in his book *Storytelling*, is particularly good at bringing Bible stories to life, and my old friend Roly Bain persuades us to look at many of them in ever more innovative ways. We can take the time to study the different ways in which people handle the Bible but we can also allow God to stir up our own creative ideas so that we present those wonderful stories in our own way. The Bible itself says, 'Do your best to win God's approval as a worker who doesn't need to be ashamed and who teaches only the true message' (2 Timothy 2:15). We owe it to ourselves and the children and adults we work with to become good students of the Bible—like avid miners, digging deep into it to unearth all the treasures it holds. But a word of warning: once we set ourselves to examine and study the word of God, we will never be the same, for the Bible is the only volume I know that reads its reader. Here's a final word for next week's assembly. Question: What colour should a Bible be? Answer: Read!

In conclusion, careful preparation, building a positive environment, making use of the resources available and communicating the truth in an engaging and professional manner should ensure that collective worship is one of the most rewarding activities we can experience.

What makes a good assembly?

Some schools wisely consult their students on the formation of a School Collective Worship Policy. Here's what the children of Saint Katherine's Church of England Primary School, Canvey Island, think makes a good assembly:

❖ A range of different types of music played when entering and leaving the hall
❖ A range of stimuli used for the assembly, such as stories, videos, visitors, poems, tapes, objects, newspapers and so on
❖ Fun songs with actions
❖ Entertaining themes and styles
❖ Use of lights or candles for atmosphere
❖ Variety of seating arrangements (in the round and so on)
❖ Audience participation
❖ Different prayers

COMPILED BY YEAR 6, JULY 2005

So far, so good. Now, we are sitting at the front and the children are starting to file in as the stirring themes of Vangelis throb softly through the speakers. How will we actually take the assembly? This is how I would do it…

I've set up a little pictorial display at the front of the hall to pique the children's interest. There's a small candle and a flower arrangement and, behind them, a big, bold, red heart cushion. I've got a box of long matches close at hand for the candle. (I find the lighters easier to use but not always reliable.) I smile reassuringly at the children as they come in and immediately try to engage them. I remind myself that they are the main reason I am here. I see that, as in most schools, the older children are at the back and the younger ones at the front.

The assembly begins. The children are all seated and the music fades. The deputy greets the children and introduces me. The children respond, 'Good morning, Mr Guest. Good morning, everybody.' I notice that some of the children are 'signing' and remember the head telling me that there are some Special Needs children in school, and two with hearing difficulties. I

don't know much BSL (British Sign Language) but at least I can say 'thank you'.

The deputy hands over to me and I speak softly but clearly to the children, endeavouring to be heard even at the back. I tell the children that I am a vicar and explain why I am here. I say that I have a story to tell them which has an animal in it, and they will have to listen carefully to spot it. I produce a red balloon from my pocket and start to model an animal, asking for hands up to guess what it might be. I make sure I get a good cross-section of contributions from back as well as front, boys as well as girls and right side as well as left side. The animal turns out to be a reindeer and the assembly is now quite excited and a little noisy. I quieten the children by asking them to look at me and waiting for them to simmer down. (There are various ways to quieten an assembly, including, as a last resort, a look of desperation flashed to the head teacher who then stands up and does it for you. You can pick up some good tips by observing the methods that experienced teachers employ.)

I say that I am going to give Mrs Matthews (the deputy, whose name I carefully remembered before the assembly began) the very hard job of looking to see who is listening best to the story, and that child will get to take the balloon animal home. I give the reindeer to Mrs Matthews and then say that we are going to try a new song. Fortunately, I am a little musical and, although I will admit to playing the piano and the accordion, I am going to do today's song 'a cappella'. It is an easily learned song from one of my assembly books, which begins quietly, gets louder and then fades away. It has the advantage of quietening the children in preparation for the story. Often, this part of the assembly will be a song chosen by the school and displayed on the screen but prior arrangement can help to find a suitable piece. It is always better to go for a song that the children know and love rather than picking a less familiar one just to fit the theme of the assembly. My song is a new one but the children get to click their fingers to it and they seem to enjoy it.

By the time the song ends, there is a hush over the assembly and I open my story book and begin 'Once upon a time...' The children are listening intently, partly because they want to win the reindeer, partly because they want to spot when the animal pops up in the narrative but mostly because it is a good story, well told. (The issue of 'blackmailing' the children with a balloon animal is controversial but all the teachers I have spoken to approve, despite being given the task of choosing a recipient.)

The story ends and I ask a few brief questions about friendship and love, linking them to the heart on the table. I light the 'prayer candle', with a small reminder about the danger of matches. I invite the children to look at the flickering flame and the heart and think about friendship. There is some quiet reflective music for about 30 seconds. As this fades softly, I invite them to close their eyes and listen to a short prayer, adding 'Amen' at the end if they wish to.

There are some sample prayers at the end of each assembly in this book. There are also some excellent prayers in a number of other assembly books, some of which are listed in the Resources section (pp. 99–100). It is a good idea to keep the prayer simple and, if in a secular school, to use 'God', 'Almighty God', 'Lord' or even 'Father' rather than 'Jesus' or 'Christ'. Sometimes it helps to personalise the prayer to emphasise individual response. I usually say the prayer and invite the children to listen, but occasionally it is possible to ask the children to say a prayer with me or after me.

I am one of those people who bemoan the decline of the Lord's Prayer, and I promised my friend Ernie that I would do all I could to encourage its increased usage in schools and children's groups. It seems to me that this is an excellent prayer that many adults remember from their school days. Although it is biblical and from the Christian tradition, it is a prayer that should not give offence to any other faith groups and is eminently suitable for every occasion. It is a prayer that unites us and goes right to the heart of our relationship with God. It is the prayer Jesus taught his disciples when they asked him how they should pray. I think it is something we should teach in our schools and whenever we have the opportunity. If you agree with me, email me at Gof4God@aol.com and let's see if we can do something about this together! A good starting point might be to buy Lucy Moore's excellent book, *The Lord's Prayer Unplugged* (Barnabas, 2004). OK, Ernie?

Back to the assembly... I blow out the candle and ask Mrs Matthews if she has found a candidate for Rudolph. The child in question retrieves the reindeer and gets a round of applause. I remind the child to give the balloon to their form teacher to be kept until the end of school. I thank everyone, using the BSL open palm to the mouth and down to signify 'thank you'. Mrs Matthews thanks me and the children clap. There are some notices. As the children leave, I give a few little waves or thumbs up and many of the children respond. A couple of them come over to me to say a private 'thank you' and one tells me they have a rabbit just like the one in the story. I am animated and interested. One little boy from Class 1 gives me a hug, which I return sensitively and in full view. I clear up my resources after the children have left and make sure the assembly area is tidy. Two children are putting away the OHP (which wasn't used) and I share a few words with them. Mrs Matthew asks me if I would like to go into the staff room for a coffee and I enthusiastically accept.

WHOLE SCHOOL ASSEMBLY

We may often find that we are asked to take an assembly for KS1 and KS2 together. This will mean presenting a relevant assembly for children aged four through to those who may soon be twelve.

We need to remember, in this case, that a primary school operates very much as a family, and the values and ethos of the school relate to all the children from the youngest to the oldest. In my experience, it is possible to deliver some good-quality collective worship without excluding the youngest ones or patronising the oldest. In this book and in *Collective Worship Unwrapped*, there are assemblies specifically prepared for both Key Stages. Also, even some of the assemblies designed for older children can be used with younger year groups.

As long as we are sensitive and professional and keep an eye on the clock, we will find that we can lead collective worship for all ages at primary school. We need to remember to focus on the 'big ones' at the back as well as the 'tinies' at the front and to involve the older ones even though they like to give the impression that they are too cool to care. We need to be careful with the words we use, but not to be over-simplistic. The checklist below shows how these principles apply to all children. I call it the ASSEMBLY check.

Checklist for assembly taking

❖ **A**rm yourself with prayer (Ephesians 6:18–19).
❖ **S**ee that you are properly prepared in every area.
❖ **S**et your watch and keep to time.
❖ **E**ngage and involve the children.
❖ **M**ake sure you include music.
❖ **B**e positive, be relevant, be fun!
❖ **L**eave a clear message.
❖ **Y**ou are God's ambassador; this is an act of worship.

So that's how we take an assembly—at least, that is how I take one. I'm not saying that this is the only way to do it or that the list of suggested actions is exhaustive. Everyone will have his or her own methods and style because everyone is unique. We mustn't hang back because we feel nervous, inadequate or ill-equipped. Too many of us put ourselves down because we have been told we are not good enough or that our 'shining' will put others in the shade. The following quotation is worth pinning to the wall of a church or school building.

Our deepest fear is not that we are inadequate. Our deepest fear is that we are powerful beyond measure. It is our light, not our darkness, that most frightens us. We ask ourselves, who am I to be brilliant, gorgeous, talented, and fabulous? Actually, who are you not to be? You are a child of God. Your playing small doesn't serve the world. There's nothing enlightened about shrinking so that other people won't feel insecure around you. We are all meant to shine, as children do. We are born to make manifest the glory of God that is within us. It's not just in some of us, it's in everyone. And as we let our own light shine, we unconsciously give other people permission to do the same. As we are liberated from our own fear, our presence automatically liberates others.

MARIANNE WILLIAMSON, *A RETURN TO LOVE*
(THORSONS, 1999)

We must take those words to heart and be a resource for God's love and power to be released in our schools and communities.

FOLLOW-UP

All the assemblies in this book include suggestions for follow-up and classroom work. There are questions and activities suitable for KS1 and KS2. Many of the assembly books listed at the end of the book also include helpful ideas for follow-up. The 'spin-offs' from assembly and collective worship can connect us with almost every aspect of the national curriculum (see www.nc.uk.net). There are particularly good connections to PSHME (Personal, Social, Health and Moral Education). In their excellent assembly books, *Kings and Monkeys* and *Ugly Bugs and Apple Trees*, Michael Catchpool and Pat Lunt include the option of PSHME ideas for follow-up with each assembly, as well as a 'general theme' and a 'Christian theme'. Gerald Haigh and Jane West, in *Assemblies Across Faiths*, also offer a number of useful ideas for a multi-faith context. Whether it is RE, PSHME, Science and Nature,

Geography, History or even Numeracy and Literacy, the primary school teacher or creative and thoughtful visitor will find numerous ideas arising from the school assembly which will carry them and a class through the rest of the school day.

One of the best kinds of follow-up is to click on to www.barnabasinschools.org.uk and follow the link to 'RE Days'. *Barnabas* RE Days offer a full day's programme to your school to explore Christianity creatively with primary-aged children through story-telling, drama, dance or music, according to the skills of the professional *Barnabas* team member. Each day provides a flexible, enjoyable and educational experience, which will unpack stories and themes from the Bible alongside contemporary life illustrations. Follow-up material is available for classroom extension work after the RE Day. *Barnabas* also offers INSET days to help schools with training.

WHAT IF IT ALL GOES WRONG?

A teacher friend of mine asked me to put this bit in! Sometimes things don't work out the way we expect. Despite our best preparation and all our careful work, something goes wrong. It can be something very minor, like losing the page in the story book (try a paper-clip marker) or being unable to light the candle (light a brand new candle before assembly to burn the wax off the wick, then blow it out), or it might be something bigger, like meeting a particularly badly behaved class, or accidentally saying something inappropriate or unrehearsed. What do we do?

First of all, we should expect that, sometimes, we will fail. Sometimes it's our fault and sometimes it isn't. Remember, the person who never did anything wrong was nailed to a cross! You should put it down to experience. I once heard a terminally ill man say that experience is what you get when you don't get what you want.

Secondly, we can minimise the possibility that things will go wrong by preparing 'back ups' and by relying as fully as we can on God.

Thirdly, when we make a mistake, we mustn't admonish ourselves. The world has enough people queuing up to do that anyway! We mustn't give up or back off or quit. We must just carry on, wiser and more experienced. We will probably find that the mistake was a lot less serious than we imagined—and, anyway, it's not how we fall down but how we get back up again that will determine our character.

Finally, we can pray—before it happens, after it happens and while it is happening.

MODEL ASSEMBLIES

I call the assemblies in this book 'model' assemblies, not because they are brilliant (even though they are!), but because they are like kits to be put together. The idea is not just to use them as they are set out but to make them your own. They can be altered and adapted to fit your own school situation and way of doing things. The missing ingredient in these models is your own imagination and creativity, which you are invited to apply.

PREPARATION TIME

Each assembly includes a brief guide to the preparation needed for the storytelling. The absolute minimum preparation time required is estimated to be between five and ten minutes, but this guideline will naturally depend on the storyteller and the availability of materials needed for props. In principle, the assemblies are designed to be 'ready-made' and everything has been kept as simple and as accessible as possible so that preparation is kept to the minimum.

Key to songs

The songs listed in each section are taken from the following books:

- ❖ **JP**: *Junior Praise*, Peter Horrobin and Greg Leavers (HarperCollins, ISBN 978 0 551 01293 6)
- ❖ **KS**: *Kidsource: Super Songs for Church and School*, Alan Price CA (Kevin Mayhew, ISBN 978 1 84003 310 6)
- ❖ **SFK**: *Songs of Fellowship for Kids* (Kingsway Music, ISBN 978 0 85476 735 9)
- ❖ **SOLW**: *Sound of Living Waters/Fresh Sounds*, Betty Pulkingham and Jeanne Harper (Hodder & Stoughton, ISBN 978 0 340 23262 0)
- ❖ **TB**: *Tinderbox: 66 Songs for Children*, Sylvia Barratt and Sheena Hodge (A&C Black, ISBN 978 0 7136-2170 9)

The three songs on the following pages are particularly successful in assemblies, because they are simple to learn, fun to sing and strongly interactive. 'Don't have a face like a coffee pot' goes down very well with very young children and the other two work well with all ages. All can be accompanied by actions, which allows more interaction and more involvement by the children.

God is good to me

Melody

God   is good to me.   God   is good to me.   He
God   is good to me.   God   is good to me.   He
God   is good to me.   God   is good to me.   He

Piano

holds   my hand,   he helps   me stand.   God   is good   to me.
holds   me tight   with all   his might.   God   is good   to me.
gives   me lips   to   eat   my chips.   God   is good   to me.

Don't have a face like a coffee pot

Reproduced with permission from *More Collective Worship Unwrapped* published by BRF 2010 (978 1 84101 664 1) www.barnabasinschools.org.uk

The remember song

Key Stage One
assemblies

The Toolshed Gang

This assembly and the next are designed primarily for Key Stage One and follow on from the six at the beginning of *Collective Worship Unwrapped*. Each assembly is strongly story-based and character-orientated and uses everyday items that can be picked up in the home, garage or garden shed as visual aids. Even in this technological age, many children still find tools fascinating and enjoy working with their hands. In these stories, the 'characters' can be produced and children can hold them—under careful supervision, of course. In addition, and to aid visual impact, you will find pictures of the main characters, which may be photocopied from pages 84–94 or downloaded from www.barnabasinschools.org.uk/morecollectiveworship.

The Toolshed Gang

Gloria Glue

STORYTELLING METHOD

Narrative with visual aids and some pupil participation

Preparation

You will need to allow yourself time to find a toolbox and, if necessary, someone who will display it. Make sure all the 'characters' are available in the box (see below).

Bible link

Romans 15:1–8, 13–14

Visual aids

- ❖ A toolbox with a selection of tools including a large hammer, a chisel, a screwdriver and a pair of pliers
- ❖ A large tube of glue
- ❖ Alternatively or, preferably, in addition, pictures of the characters to show or project

> **Helpful hints:** Be very careful when allowing the children to handle the tools, especially the chisel and the pliers. The chisel should be masked in a case and children should be discouraged from opening and shutting the pliers. Take the opportunity to stress the importance of tools and the dangers of using them improperly. This could be a good opportunity to involve the school caretaker or maintenance operative or even an appropriate and available parent who works with tools.

Main themes

Friendship and coming together

Further topics covered
Encouragement and inspiration

Prayer

Lord, help us to remember the importance of sticking together and working things out, no matter how hard that may be. Thank you for showing us that, if we listen to your instructions, we can make a new start. Amen

Songs

Thank you for my friends (TB)
Bind us together, Lord (JP)
Jesus put this song into our hearts (KS)

FOLLOW-UP

This is an opportunity to discuss what happens when we have arguments and friendships break up; how we resolve conflict or encourage others when they feel like giving up. You could try asking some of the following questions: What tools were mentioned in today's story and how were they feeling? Do you feel that you are like any of the tools in the story? Which ones and why? What does Gloria Glue remind you of? How do you feel when you have an argument with one of your friends? What do you do when you feel like giving up? Who can you talk to when you feel cross or sad? How hard is it to decide to make a new start?

You could spend some time encouraging the children to comment on the positive qualities of classmates. This could be extended into a project, drawing or painting pictures of each other with comments like 'Lisa is good at... Bradley is my friend because... Lauren is great in this class because...' The pictures could be made into school posters or tea towels.

Once upon a time, not so long ago, in a shed at the bottom of the garden, was a toolbox. I don't know its name but it was big and it was strong and it had many tools inside it. It belonged to the Master Builder and he loved it and all the tools inside it.

Four of the tools were particularly important. They were good friends who did a lot of work together. Let's meet them, shall we?

As you introduce the four main characters, you can take them out of the toolbox and/or show them on the screen.

First, there was Billy the Big Hammer. He was strong and liked working but was inclined to be a bit hard-headed. He was also a lot bigger than Sally the Small Hammer, who was only used for the more delicate jobs. Next there was Clara the Chisel. She was tall and slim but also had rather a sharp tongue. After her came Sammy the Screwdriver. He could turn himself to most jobs and was particularly useful at getting in and out of scrapes. Finally, there was Paula the Pliers. Although she was rather short and fat, once she got a grip on something, she never let go!

Sammy the Screwdriver was in a whirl; he felt like his head was spinning! He had had such a busy day, he didn't know what to turn to next. He lay by the side of the toolbox and everything seemed to go round and round. 'I just couldn't do another thing,' he wheezed. 'I don't think I can ever do another thing. I'm completely worn out!' He looked round for his friends.

Squinting through the gloom, he was just able to make out Clara the Chisel leaning against the edge of the toolbox. 'Clara!' called Sammy. 'Come over and cheer me up. I feel so tired and poorly.' There was no answer. 'Clara!' called Sammy again. 'Is everything all right? Where are the others? Where's Paula? What's happened to Billy?'

Finally Clara moved and, as she came over to Sammy, he saw that she had a large misshapen bruise on her head. 'Don't talk to me about Billy!'

snapped Clara. 'I am never speaking to that hammer again! Do you know what he did? He hit me! And I don't mean softly. Just look at my head.' Sammy looked again and, as he peered closely at her, he could see that Clara had been crying. She hardly ever did that.

'I'm not staying around here to be hit,' exclaimed Clara. 'Paula and I have been talking. We're leaving. We're off to join another toolbox. She's fed up with Oily Fred oozing all over her when she has the slightest creak, and if I have to hear that Timmy Tilecutter squeaking at me just once more, I'll scream!'

Sammy didn't say anything. He was too tired. But he didn't get much sleep that night as he lay in the toolbox and listened to a lot of the tools complaining about how tired and depressed they felt. Billy wasn't talking to Clara, Ritchie Rasp was starting to needle everybody, Pontifex the Power Saw was on a go-slow and there didn't seem to be any sign of Oily Fred. Sammy knew how everybody felt. The trouble was, talking about it to the other tools didn't seem to make him feel any better.

The following morning, he lay on the bench feeling more wretched than ever before. He had just decided he might as well pack up and go off with Clara and Paula when a small sticky piece of paper floated down from above and landed on his nose. 'Gloria Innecselsis: Glue you can really stick with!' he read on the paper.

'Gloria?' thought Sammy. 'I don't think I've met her before.' He looked at the bottom of the label and read the instructions. His dad Stanley had always drummed into him the need to read the instructions before starting any job. They were very interesting and before long he decided to go and look for Gloria Glue. Billy the Big Hammer was sulking and wouldn't come with him. Most of the other tools were either too busy or too cross. In the end, Sally the Small Hammer agreed to join him.

It was a long trip to the end of the bench but somehow Sammy didn't feel as tired or depressed as he had felt earlier. Sally didn't say much but at

Reproduced with permission from *More Collective Worship Unwrapped* published by BRF 2010 (978 1 84101 664 1) www.barnabasinschools.org.uk

least she wasn't complaining and grumbling like the other tools.

'What's that?' she said suddenly as they approached the very end of the workbench.

At the end of the bench, next to a big bag of nails, sat a large tube with a small, round cap and a big curly tail. As it turned towards Sammy and Sally, they saw that it had a big smiley face on one side.

'Hello there!' said Gloria Glue to the two tools. 'Nice to meet you. I'm Gloria Glue. Gloria Glue, Gloria True, sticking together with me and you!' And she gave them both a great big grin.

'I see you've found my label, Sammy,' said Gloria Glue, 'and it looks like you've started to read the instructions, too, or you wouldn't be here. I guess you know that the Master Builder has given me the job of helping things to stick together. So tell me, what can I do for you?'

So Sammy the Screwdriver (with a little help from Sally the Small Hammer) started to explain how sad it was in the toolshed just at the moment, with all the tools bickering and everyone feeling so depressed. Gloria was really helpful. She pointed out the instructions on her label once again and reminded Sammy and Sally how important it was for all the tools to work together and to stop saying bad things all the time.

'Like it says on the label,' she smiled, 'you've got to make sure the things you want to stick together are clean and dry. No rough and uneven bits, and certainly no dirt or mess.'

Sammy and Sally promised they would go back and tell all the other tools about the importance of sticking together, no matter what. They thanked Gloria for her advice.

'That's what I'm here for,' said Gloria Glue. 'I'm just reminding you to follow the Master Builder's instructions. Any time you need me to bring people together, just call. Gloria Glue, Gloria True, sticking together with me and you! Now come on guys—how about a group hug?'

'Gloria Glue, Gloria True, sticking together with me and you!' sang Sammy and Sally together as they set off back along the workbench. They were absolutely determined to make a new start and, whatever it took, to encourage all the tools to stick together!

Reproduced with permission from *More Collective Worship Unwrapped* published by BRF 2010 (978 1 84101 664 1) www.barnabasinschools.org.uk

The Toolshed Gang

Jimmy the Jigsaw

STORYTELLING METHOD

Narrative with visual aids and some pupil participation

Preparation

You will need to allow yourself time to find a toolbox and, if necessary, someone who will display it. Make sure all the 'characters' are available in the box (see below).

Bible link

Colossians 3:5–10, 12–17

Visual aids

❖ A toolbox with a selection of tools including a large hammer, a chisel, a screwdriver and a pair of pliers
❖ A jigsaw
❖ Alternatively or, preferably, in addition, pictures of the characters to show or project

> **Helpful hints: See page 23 for safety advice on handling tools.**

Main themes

Telling lies, name calling and bullying

Further topics covered
Conflict resolution and character building

Prayer

Father God, show me every day the importance of telling the truth and owning up when I do wrong. Help me not to tell lies or call people bad names. Thank you, God. Amen

Songs

I want to be a tree that's bearing fruit (KS)
So if you think you're standing firm (KS)
Jesus, Jesus, here I am (KS)

FOLLOW-UP

This assembly is quite hard-hitting and deals with a number of highly emotive issues. Be prepared to face these issues sensitively with the children. You could ask the following questions: How did Paula feel when Jimmy called her names? The story says she was 'rather short and fat', so why was it wrong for Jimmy to call her that? How did Paula feel when she was accused of stealing? What did her friends do to try to help? Why did Jimmy say he was the Master Builder's favourite? Why was he so unkind to Paula? Why did he tell lies? Do you know any bullies? What do they do or say? How can you stand up to bullies? (Emphasise the importance of telling a teacher, parent or trusted grown-up rather than trying to get your own back.) How hard is it to tell the truth or to own up when you do something wrong? Was Pontifex the Power Saw good or bad in his behaviour? What would you say to Jimmy to help him to change?

End this session by emphasising school policies on bullying, name-calling, truth-telling and respect for others.

Once upon a time, not so long ago, in a shed at the bottom of the garden, was a toolbox. I don't know its name but it was big and it was strong and it had many tools inside it. It belonged to the Master Builder and he loved it and all the tools inside it.

Four of the tools were particularly important. They were good friends who did a lot of work together. Let's meet them, shall we?

As you introduce the four main characters, you can take them out of the toolbox and/or show them on the screen.

First, there was Billy the Big Hammer. He was strong and liked working but was inclined to be a bit hard-headed. He was also a lot bigger than Sally the Small Hammer, who was only used for the more delicate jobs. Next there was Clara the Chisel. She was tall and slim but also had rather a sharp tongue. After her came Sammy the Screwdriver. He could turn himself to most jobs and was particularly useful at getting in and out of scrapes. Finally, there was Paula the Pliers. Although she was rather short and fat, once she got a grip on something, she never let go!

'You're lazy, you're too fat and you smell funny!' said Jimmy the Jigsaw to Paula the Pliers as she sat by the toolbox after a hard day's work.

You could show a jigsaw at this point and carefully point out that in this case it is a type of saw and not a puzzle that you put together on a table!

Jimmy the Jigsaw had only been in the toolshed for a few weeks but some of the tools were quickly beginning to realise that he wasn't really very nice. He'd been niggling Paula for some days now. He often had a sharp or unkind word to say, but usually when nobody else was listening.

'You're not nearly as clever as me,' said Jimmy unkindly as Paula sat up with tears in her eyes. 'I can go into all kinds of places you can't, and I'm MB's favourite!'

'MB?' sniffed Paula. 'Who's that?'

'M… B… Master Builder. Don't you even know that, Potty Paula?' sneered Jimmy and he pushed her with his sharp blade. 'Well, I guess only the special tools call him MB.' He laughed in her face and went off.

Billy and Clara found Paula sobbing by herself later on. 'He's so nasty to me,' she told them, 'and I've never done anything to him!'

'Dry your eyes, Paula,' said Clara kindly to her friend. 'We have to stand up to bullies. We're your friends. We'll stick with you.'

'Don't worry, Paula,' said Billy the Big Hammer. 'I'll have a word with Ritchie and Reggie. They'll sort Jimmy out!'

Just then, Sammy the Screwdriver jumped down beside them. 'Have you heard the news? There's quite a fuss going on in the toolshed. Someone's taken the Master Builder's apron and he can't get any work done!' Paula's problems were quite forgotten as all the tools began to talk excitedly about the problem. Nothing like this had ever happened before.

Later that day, Oily Fred gathered all the tools together and asked if anyone had seen the Master Builder's apron. It had been taken from the door earlier that day. 'I bet Jimmy's nicked it,' whispered Clara to Paula as they stood together. 'It would be just like him!'

Paula took a deep breath. She remembered the need to stand up to bullies. 'Why don't you ask Jimmy if he's seen it, Oily Fred?' she shouted out suddenly. All the other tools turned and looked at her.

'I haven't seen it at all, Mr Oily Fred, sir,' said Jimmy in his nicest voice. 'Why, I've been here in the toolbox all day with my friend Mr Power Saw, haven't I, Ponty?' He turned to the large and impressive figure of Pontifex the Power Saw, who nodded in confirmation. 'I wouldn't dream of touching the Master's apron!'

Just then, the tall figure of Ritchie Rasp pushed through the crowd. ''Ere, Oily!' he called. 'Look

Reproduced with permission from *More Collective Worship Unwrapped* published by BRF 2010 (978 1 84101 664 1) www.barnabasinschools.org.uk

what Reggie's found.' And he held up a piece of creased and dirty material. The Master's apron!

'We nearly missed it,' explained Ritchie, 'but Reggie and me, we don't give up easily. We got an inside tip-off, see? We found it, shoved in a corner, in her quarters!' And he turned suddenly and pointed to Paula.

Paula the Pliers was stunned. 'I'm so disappointed in you,' wheezed Oily Fred. 'I thought you were such a good pair of pliers.' He turned sadly away to take the apron back to the Master Builder. Paula burst into tears.

Many of the other tools wouldn't talk to her after that. Sammy, Billy and Clara tried to console her but it was no good. She took to sitting on her own and was often unavailable for work.

Later that week, Jimmy the Jigsaw found her on the edge of the workbench, all alone. She tried to move away but Jimmy stopped her, blocking her path with his long sharp blade. 'Leave me alone!' cried Paula. 'I've never done anything to hurt you.'

'Really?' said Jimmy, cruelly giving Paula's little green legs a sharp nip. 'What about accusing me of stealing the other day? And all the time it was you—you bad, lazy, fat, smelly little pair of pliers. Why don't you do all of us a favour and jump off the bench?' And he looked down suggestively into the depths below.

'But it wasn't me, it wasn't!' complained Paula. 'I didn't take anything. I don't know how the Master's apron got into my corner.'

'But I do, little fat Potty Paula,' said Jimmy in his nastiest voice. 'I do! You see, I took it from the back of the door when MB was washing his hands. I took it and I put it into your corner, and now I've got Ponty's word I was with him all the time, and he's the biggest tool in the box. Nobody will believe you and nobody wants to be your friend, and if you tell anybody anything bad about me you'll wish you'd never been made!' And he jabbed Paula's legs once more to make his point.

'Well, I think we've heard enough,' came a funny squeaky voice, and Oily Fred stepped out from behind the toolbox. 'Jimmy! I need a word with you!'

Jimmy gave a lopsided smile. 'Me, Mr Oily Fred, sir? I was just sitting here trying to cheer Paula up. She's so sad.'

'The game's up, Jimmy,' said Billy, stepping out to join Oily Fred and then being joined by the other two friends. 'Pontifex the Power Saw confessed everything,' explained Sammy. 'Paula's off the hook.'

Jimmy the Jigsaw was taken away snarling and swearing and wasn't seen again in the toolbox by any of the other tools. I'd like to think he made a public apology to Paula but I don't think he ever did.

Clara the Chisel comforted Paula later that day. 'You were great,' she said to her friend. 'You stood up to a bully and told the truth, and that's what matters!'

I think she was right, don't you?

Reproduced with permission from *More Collective Worship Unwrapped* published by BRF 2010 (978 1 84101 664 1) www.barnabasinschools.org.uk

The amazing adventures of Mrs Bitsy

The 'Mrs Bitsy' stories that follow seek to do two things. First of all, they allow younger and less confident children to have a 'proxy' for expressing their feelings. Many schools today have a cuddly toy—often a teddy bear—that goes on trips with the school or class. It might even go home with pupils and on holiday with them. The teddy will be photographed and drawn and children will be asked how the teddy feels in response to various stimuli. The children will then often express their own feelings without embarrassment.

Secondly, these assemblies are a response to several teachers who have asked me for more stories from the life of Jesus as portrayed in the New Testament. Mrs Bitsy adds a new dimension, which, I hope, will commend them particularly to KS1. In addition, many of these stories return again and again to the theme of 'friendship'. This, above all, was the theme that primary school teachers asked me to include in the book.

Mrs Bitsy, by the way, is the invention of my daughter Hannah. This motherly teddy was named and claimed by Hannah when she was an infant, many years ago.

Mrs Bitsy and the magic wedding

STORYTELLING METHOD

Narrative with optional visual aids

Preparation

Take time to read the story through and practise retelling it in your own words.

Bible link

John 2:1–12

Visual aids

❖ A shopping basket with some groceries
❖ A bottle of wine or champagne and a flagon or goblet

Helpful hints: You can dramatise the story or tell it straight. You could use visual aids or just tell the story from a large book. This is a good story to involve the children if you can get volunteers to play some of the characters. Young children enjoy dressing up (some older ones, too!) so you might include some simple costumes.

Main themes

Being special and positive transformation

Further topics covered
Peer pressure and feeling overlooked

Prayer

Dear Lord, help me to know that I am special. Help me to remember this when I feel overlooked or forgotten. Thank you for loving me. Amen

Songs

If I were a butterfly (KS)
You may think I'm so young (KS)
I am a new creation (KS)

FOLLOW-UP

Use your 'Mrs Bitsy' teddy bear or similar cuddly toy to encourage the children to share their feelings. How did Mrs Bitsy feel about being invited to a wedding? Have you ever been to a wedding? What was it like? Why was Ben so sad and cross? Do you know anyone who ever felt like that? What did Mrs Bitsy say to help Ben and stop him running away? Mrs Bitsy and Ben did lots of fun things together. What fun things do you do with your friends? What made Rachel's wedding really amazing? How do you think ordinary things can become special?

You might like to encourage the children to make lists of things they think are ordinary and things they think are special.

Mrs Bitsy was a bear—just a small brown furry teddy bear. But Mrs Bitsy was no ordinary teddy bear. Oh no! Mrs Bitsy was special. Mrs Bitsy loved everyone and everyone loved her. To you and me she looked like an ordinary bear, with a little red shawl and small round button eyes, but Mrs Bitsy had some amazing adventures. Would you like to hear one of them? You would? Well, listen carefully and I'll begin.

It was Mrs Bitsy's shopping day. She'd set out early that morning, before the sun had climbed too high in the sky, and taken her big basket down to the village market. She'd managed to buy some juicy fruit and some nice fresh vegetables as well as a big pot of her favourite runny honey and a giant sack of oats for porridge. She'd also ordered a new tea service for Rachel, her next-door neighbour, who was to be married to Thomas the carpenter in ten days' time. It was a while since Mrs Bitsy had been to a wedding and she was feeling very excited.

As she started out on a short cut across the fields to her cottage, she heard a snuffling noise coming from behind one of the bushes. When she investigated further, she found young Benjamin Barjonas, sitting on a fallen log and looking very sorry for himself. Ben was Rachel's youngest brother.

'What are you doing here, Ben?' asked Mrs Bitsy. 'Shouldn't you be at school by now?'

Ben looked up and Mrs Bitsy could see where two lines of tears had stained his face. 'I'm not going,' he said unhappily. 'I'm going away and I'm not coming back. Ever!'

Mrs Bitsy put down her heavy shopping basket and sat on the log next to Ben. 'Whatever has brought this on, young Ben?' said Mrs Bitsy, passing him an enormous pink spotted handkerchief to wipe his eyes. 'What will your mum and dad think if you run away?'

'They don't care,' sniffed Ben. 'They wouldn't even notice I'd gone. They're too busy sorting out the wedding. Rachel's getting a special wedding dress and Ethan's practising his playing for the service and Reuben is planning the food and Dad's

out every day getting extra fish in. Mum never stops talking about the wedding. I made a collage at school for her last week and she didn't even notice. I'm not important enough!'

'Everyone's important, Ben,' said Mrs Bitsy, kindly. 'We're all special in one way or another.'

'I'm not!' said Ben crossly. 'I can't do sums and I can't do spelling. Everyone at school's cleverer than me. So I'm going away. I don't suppose anyone will care.'

'I will,' said Mrs Bitsy. 'You're my best friend, Ben. Who will I have to tell me their adventures after school? Who will help me with the washing when I'm busy, or catch old Mr Josephson's cat when it gets out, or help me count the stars from the top of Olive Grove Hill on a winter's night? You're important to me, Benjamin, and you know what? I think you're important to a lot of other people, too.'

Mrs Bitsy didn't get home as early as she expected that day, and Ben didn't run away from home. Just over a week later, they were both at Thomas' and Rachel's wedding.

The couple looked lovely, and they adored the tea set Mrs Bitsy gave them. Ben looked very smart in a set of new clothes that his mum had made, and was very busy carrying the food and drink to all the guests. There was a lot of attention focused on one guest in particular—Jesus from Nazareth, who many called the Great Rabbi. He was there with his mother, Mary, and a few of their friends from Cana. Mary was sitting chatting to Mrs Bitsy when Ben rushed up to inform them that all the special wedding wine had run out and there was nothing left to drink!

'Oh, dearie dear!' said Mrs Bitsy to Jesus' mother. 'Mr and Mrs Barjonas will be so upset. They did so want Rachel's wedding to be special.'

Mary said nothing but walked over to where Jesus was talking to some of the other guests. Then, after a moment, she called the waiters over. Some time later, Benjamin appeared at Mrs Bitsy's side with a large cup full of wine. Mrs Bitsy took a little sip. 'Why, Ben,' she exclaimed, 'this is delicious!

Reproduced with permission from *More Collective Worship Unwrapped* published by BRF 2010 (978 1 84101 664 1) www.barnabasinschools.org.uk

I thought you said all the wine was gone.'

'It's the Great Rabbi,' replied Ben. 'I think he has done some magic. He got all the washing water out of the kitchen—about 600 litres, Reuben said—and he's turned it into wine!'

'It's not magic,' smiled Mrs Bitsy. 'Jesus can do that because he is so special. It's like I said to you last week. We're all special in one way or another. Jesus can take something ordinary, like washing water, and turn it into the best wine. And guess what, Ben? He can take ordinary people and make them special too!'

Ben gave Mrs Bitsy his biggest smile. 'I still think it's a magic wedding, Mrs Bitsy. Well magic!'

Mrs Bitsy and the hole in the ceiling

STORYTELLING METHOD

Narrative with optional visual aids

 ## Preparation

Take time to read the story through and practise retelling it in your own words.

 ## Bible link

Mark 2:1–12

 ## Visual aids

If you wanted, you could use some pictures of houses from first-century Palestine or show a ceiling with a big hole in it.

> Helpful hints: This assembly might offer you the chance to talk about friends and how important they are in school. You could talk to the children about how God is your friend (if he is!) and how he wants to be friends with them.

 ## Main themes

Friendship and helping others

Further topics covered
Perseverance and faith

 ## Prayer

Father God, thank you for my friends. Thank you for everyone who helps me. Please help me to be a good and helpful friend, too. Amen

 ## Songs

One more step along the world I go (JP)
I'm accepted, I'm forgiven (KS)
Thank you for my friends (TB)

FOLLOW-UP

Once again, using the 'Mrs Bitsy' teddy, encourage the children to talk about friendship and helping others. How did Mrs Bitsy feel when she lay awake in bed? Did she feel frightened by all the noises? How did she feel about missing the trip with Ben? What did Ben do to help? Why do you think Thomas and Ben's mum offered to help? Why were so many people crammed into the house to hear Jesus talk? What was it like for the crippled man and his friends? Do you know anyone who needs to be helped because they are disabled?

You might like to launch a project on friendship—how we make friends and what constitutes a good friend. Make reference to any school values that are appropriate.

Mrs Bitsy was a bear—just a small brown furry teddy bear. But Mrs Bitsy was no ordinary teddy bear. Oh no! Mrs Bitsy was special. Mrs Bitsy loved everyone and everyone loved her. To you and me she looked like an ordinary bear, with a little red shawl and small round button eyes, but Mrs Bitsy had some amazing adventures. Would you like to hear one of them? You would? Well, listen carefully and I'll begin.

It was the middle of the night and Mrs Bitsy should have been asleep, tucked up in her big warm bed, nice and toasty! But Mrs Bitsy couldn't get to sleep. Old Mr Josephson's cat was up on the roof, complaining to the moon, the wind was blowing loudly through the trees and under the eaves of the houses, and Mrs Bitsy's cottage seemed to be full of strange creaks and groans. Mrs Bitsy knew she had a lot to do that week and worried about how it could all be done in time. She tossed and turned but couldn't settle. The cat had stopped yowling, but now the rain had started, and the noise of the pat-patter on the roof was not helping at all. To make matters worse, a huge drop of water fell from the ceiling right on to Mrs Bitsy's big brown nose. There was a large hole right above her bed and it was getting bigger!

Poor Mrs Bitsy had to go downstairs and curl up on the kitchen chair. She didn't get much sleep that night and, in the morning, in addition to all her other chores, there was a hole in the ceiling to mend. The trouble was, even standing on her very tippytoes, Mrs Bitsy couldn't reach it. She was just hanging out her wet bedclothes on the washing line when the kitchen gate burst open and Benjamin Barjonas from next door ran in.

'The Great Rabbi is visiting Capernaum!' he shouted excitedly. 'Reuben says everyone's going to hear him. Would you like to come, Mrs Bitsy? All my friends are going from school but you're my best friend, Mrs Bitsy, so I thought I'd ask you.'

'Well, that's very kind of you, Ben,' said Mrs Bitsy, 'but I'm afraid it's a very difficult time for me. I have a big hole in my ceiling and nothing to mend it with.

I can't even reach the hole and I don't know anyone else who's tall enough. Besides, I'll have no time to go to the shops if I go to Capernaum with you, and I still have a lot of water to mop up in my bedroom. I'm sorry, Ben. I expect there will be other times.' She gave Ben a big hug and the young boy went back home.

Later that morning, Mrs Bitsy stood in her bedroom, surveying the mess from last night's rain. It was still windy and that hole wasn't getting any smaller. Just then, she heard a shout from downstairs and up the steps came Ben Barjonas, followed by Thomas the carpenter and the tallest man Mrs Bitsy had ever seen. They seemed to be carrying wood and tools.

'This is Thomas' business partner, Heman,' said Ben. 'They've come to mend your roof. Heman is really good at the tall jobs, as you can see.'

'Couldn't leave a friend in need, Mrs Bitsy,' smiled Thomas as he set his hammer, nails, chisel and saw out on the floor. 'Not after all you've done for me and Rachel.'

'Mum says she can take care of all the drying and clearing up for you, Mrs Bitsy,' said Ben. 'She has to stay in anyway to look after Mr Josephson's cat while he's away at his brother's in Capernaum. Oh, and she says, don't worry about the shopping. She's still got lots of food left over from the wedding. Look, she's packed us both some lunch for our trip. You are going to come, aren't you?'

Little tears formed in the corners of Mrs Bitsy's eyes and she nodded. 'Thank you, Ben,' she beamed. 'I'll just get my shawl.'

It was a great day at Capernaum, even though Mrs Bitsy and Ben and all their friends were so squashed by the crowd that had gone to hear Jesus, they could hardly see! Mrs Bitsy managed to get up on a windowsill in the small house that everyone had crammed into, and Ben had climbed on his dad's shoulders to get a better look. Half way through Jesus' talk, an amazing thing happened. A big chunk of plaster fell down, just missing Jesus. As everyone looked up, they saw a hole being made in the ceiling, getting bigger and bigger! But it wasn't wind and rain that were doing the damage—it was four people who had brought a disabled man to meet Jesus. Because they couldn't get through the crowd, they had carried him up to the roof and were now lowering him through on a stretcher!

Jesus was brilliant. He spoke to the man and told him all his sins were forgiven. Then he healed the man and he stood up, completely well, picked up his stretcher and carried it home.

'Wow!' said Ben to Mrs Bitsy afterwards. 'That was well cool! I guess they'll need Thomas and Heman to mend their ceiling, too. Wasn't that amazing? A disabled man lowered through the ceiling!'

'Yes,' smiled Mrs Bitsy. 'And wasn't it a good thing that he had his friends to help him?'

Reproduced with permission from *More Collective Worship Unwrapped* published by BRF 2010 (978 1 84101 664 1) www.barnabasinschools.org.uk

The amazing adventures of Mrs Bitsy

Mrs Bitsy and the shared lunch

STORYTELLING METHOD

Narrative with optional visual aids

Preparation

Take time to read the story through and practise retelling it in your own words.

Bible link

John 6:3–13

Main themes

Sharing and friendship

Further topics covered
Hospitality and service

Visual aids

❖ Five bread rolls and two fish (these could be real, plastic or just pictures)
❖ A red shawl or blanket to wrap the rolls and fish in

> Helpful hints: Don't forget to dramatise the narrative. Imagine Mrs Bitsy and Ben, Jesus and the crowd of hungry people.

Prayer

Dear God, thank you for the food we have to eat each day. Help us to share what we have and to be kind to others. Amen

Songs

I'm not alone (SFK)
What a friend we have in Jesus (JP)
This little light of mine (KS)

FOLLOW-UP

You could start with a sharing time or circle time. If you have a cuddly toy or a 'Mrs Bitsy' bear of your own, it could be passed around the children. Encourage them to express how they feel about sharing and what it might be like to have little when someone else has more. What happens when a friend's packed lunch has nicer sandwiches than yours? How did Mrs Bitsy feel when she realised she had to give up all her food and even share her breakfast? How did Ben feel when he realised there was nobody to get him any food? What can we do in school when other people don't have as much as we do? How can we help children in other countries who don't have clean water or enough food or a dry safe place to live?

You might take this opportunity to share news of any developing world projects you know about. You could also talk about fish and bread and develop aspects of the curriculum that would lead to projects on fishing, baking and other kinds of food production. Encourage lots of drawing and colouring.

Mrs Bitsy was a bear—just a small brown furry teddy bear. But Mrs Bitsy was no ordinary teddy bear. Oh no! Mrs Bitsy was special. Mrs Bitsy loved everyone and everyone loved her. To you and me she looked like an ordinary bear, with a little red shawl and small round button eyes, but Mrs Bitsy had some amazing adventures. Would you like to hear one of them? You would? Well, listen carefully and I'll begin.

One fine day, Mrs Bitsy was sitting at her kitchen table finishing her breakfast (it was her favourite—rich thick porridge with lots of runny honey) when there came a knock at the kitchen door. 'Who could that be at this time of the day?' thought Mrs Bitsy. She opened the door to find her next-door neighbour, young Benjamin Barjonas, wearing a very sad face. 'Come in, come in,' said Mrs Bitsy, 'and tell me what's the matter.'

'My friends and I are going to hear the Great Rabbi,' explained Ben. 'You know, the carpenter from Nazareth. He's coming back to Galilee today and we're leaving any moment now, and I haven't had any breakfast, and my dad's gone out on the early morning fishing trip, and Mum's not feeling well, and I haven't got anything for my lunch and, oh, Mrs Bitsy, I'm going to be ever so hungry!'

'Hush now, young man,' said Mrs Bitsy kindly. 'You sit right down here and finish up this porridge and I'll see what I can find for you in my larder.' Mrs Bitsy left Ben eating the remains of her breakfast and peeked into the larder. Truth to tell, Mrs Bitsy had not been to the shops for a few days and there was very little to be seen—just a few bread rolls she'd baked yesterday and a couple of sardines she was saving for tonight's supper. If she gave him those, what would be left for her?

'Don't your friends have any lunch you could share, Ben?' said Mrs Bitsy.

Ben lifted his face out of the porridge bowl. 'No, Mrs Bitsy. They said they expected some of the families to be at the gathering with some food of their own. But I haven't got anything.'

Mrs Bitsy made her mind up. She packed the five rolls and two sardines tightly in her shawl and gave them to Ben. She could always go to the shops later.

'Now let me wash that porridge off your face before you go,' said Mrs Bitsy, and she fetched a flannel. 'Don't go eating all that food yourself,' she called after him as Ben darted out of the door. 'Don't forget to share!'

Well, it was the end of the afternoon by the time Mrs Bitsy got to the shops, and the grocer had sold nearly all his produce. She had just sat down to a very late supper when there came a tap at the door. Young Ben was there once more.

'I just came to bring your shawl back, Mrs Bitsy,' he said as he handed it to her. 'It's quite clean—see.'

'Sit down a moment, Ben,' replied Mrs Bitsy, pulling out a chair for him. 'How did you get on? Did you see Jesus, the Great Rabbi?

'Oh yes, Mrs Bitsy,' said Ben. 'I did see him, and what's more—he spoke to me!' Mrs Bitsy nodded and a big smile lit up her face.

'There were loads of people at the gathering,' explained Ben. 'Thousands, I should think! None of my friends' families seemed to have brought any food with them and I didn't see anyone else with packed lunches, either. I had four friends so I thought we could have a roll each, but then Uncle Andrew came over to me—he's one of Jesus' special friends now, you know—and said the Great Rabbi wanted to talk to me. Me, Mrs Bitsy, me!

'Jesus was very nice. We sat down together and he asked if he could share my lunch. He said he really liked sardines. I told him I had a friend who said it was important to share (that's you, Mrs Bitsy) and he took my lunch and said a special blessing prayer. You know, like the one Father says at the sabbath meal. I thought it would just be us eating my lunch, but Jesus and his friends and me, we shared my lunch with everyone, Mrs Bitsy. I don't know if sharing my lunch made other people share theirs, too, or if Jesus did some kind of special miracle (he's good at those, you know), but everyone there had enough to eat—even my friends, and they're well greedy! What do you think of that?'

'I think it's wonderful,' said Mrs Bitsy. 'Wonderful! Now, Ben, would you like to stay and share some of my supper?'

Reproduced with permission from *More Collective Worship Unwrapped* published by BRF 2010 (978 1 84101 664 1) www.barnabasinschools.org.uk

Mrs Bitsy and the noisy beggar

STORYTELLING METHOD

Narrative with optional visual aids

Preparation

Take time to read the story through and practise retelling it in your own words.

Bible link

Mark 10:46–52

Visual aids

If it seems appropriate, some visual aids connected with blindness, such as a 'talking book', a white stick, some glasses and some examples of Braille.

Helpful hints: The subject of blindness (and, indeed, any special need) should be handled sensitively, especially if there are visually impaired children in the school. RNIB should be able to offer helpful advice.

Main themes

Perseverance, determination and special needs

Further topics covered
Helping others and learning

Prayer

Dear God, please help all who find it difficult to see or hear or speak. Help me to work hard, to help others and to be determined to do my best. Amen

Songs

The steadfast love of the Lord never ceases (JP)
God is so good (KS)
Make me a channel of your peace (JP)

FOLLOW-UP

Pass your bear or cuddly toy around and talk about the story. Why was Ben so bored? Why did Mrs Bitsy want to help him with his homework? How did blind Bartimaeus feel when people ignored him or didn't help him when he asked? Why was Bartimaeus so noisy? (Make a distinction between times when it is important to be noisy and when we should be quiet—for example, at sports events as opposed to in the classroom.) Why is it important never to give up?

Discuss some examples of famous people who have overcome difficulties (particularly disability) to achieve their goals, such as Helen Keller, Danny Crates or Tanni Grey-Thompson. Consider a project on special needs or on the joy of reading.

Mrs Bitsy was a bear—just a small brown furry teddy bear. But Mrs Bitsy was no ordinary teddy bear. Oh no! Mrs Bitsy was special. Mrs Bitsy loved everyone and everyone loved her. To you and me she looked like an ordinary bear, with a little red shawl and small round button eyes, but Mrs Bitsy had some amazing adventures. Would you like to hear one of them? You would? Well, listen carefully and I'll begin.

It was a lovely day in Cana. Mrs Bitsy was sitting in her back garden with young Ben Barjonas, listening to him reading. The late afternoon sun was still warm on their backs and the crickets were chirruping merrily in the trees. Ben often came round to Mrs Bitsy's house to get help with his homework, and the kind motherly bear was always glad to see his latest school project or listen to his reading. But today Benjamin was struggling. His mind wasn't really on his work. He was thinking of playing down by the lake with his friends, hunting for crabs in the rock pools or helping his dad with the fishing nets. He gave a big sigh, leaned back on the grass and squinted through his fingers at the fading sunshine.

'Homework's boring,' he said at last. 'Boring, boring, boring.' And he started singing, 'S'boring, s'boring, the old man is snoring. He bumped his head on the end of the bed and he couldn't get up in the morning.'

'Come along now, Ben,' protested Mrs Bitsy. 'Your mother wouldn't thank me for letting you get away without reading at least six pages today. You know your teacher says you don't read enough.'

'But I've had enough reading,' complained Ben. 'My eyes hurt and my head aches. And anyway, the words are too hard to read. I want to go and play with my friends.'

'I've got a friend who would be glad to see what you're reading,' said Mrs Bitsy. 'He was a bit like you but he wasn't a Barjonas, he was a Bartimaeus. He tended to be a bit noisy too, but he had good reason to try to make people notice him, because he was a beggar and needed people to help him.'

Ben sat up. 'Why did he beg, Mrs Bitsy?' asked Ben. 'Why didn't he work like my dad or like Thomas the carpenter?'

'He couldn't work,' Mrs Bitsy explained. 'You see, my friend Bartimaeus was blind. His eyes often felt sore, but not because he was tired of reading. He couldn't see anything—or anyone. His head often ached, but not because of homework. It was because, if there was no one to guide him, he would bump into things or fall over.'

'Gosh,' said Ben, 'it must be very frustrating being blind. What happened to your friend?'

'Well,' went on Mrs Bitsy, 'Barty had no family to guide him and very few friends to help him, either. Each day he would sit by the side of the road and ask people for money or food so that he could live. Each night he would try his best to find somewhere warm and dry where he could sleep. But it's not easy trying to do everything by touch or having to rely only on your hearing. I remember he used to shout a lot, but only so that people would know where he was and maybe help him. I think he was quite lonely, too. One day he overheard some people talking about the Great Rabbi and the amazing things he did.'

'Hey, Mrs Bitsy, we've seen Jesus do amazing things too, haven't we? If he went to Barty's town, maybe he would help him.'

'Yes we have, Ben, and yes he did,' replied Mrs Bitsy, 'but try to listen to the story.'

'Sorry, Mrs Bitsy.'

'Well,' Mrs Bitsy went on, 'somehow Bartimaeus got to hear that Jesus was coming to his town that week and he became determined to meet him. But just imagine, Ben, how hard it is for a blind man to manage that. First, he had to find out on what day Jesus was coming and what road he would be travelling along and at what time. He couldn't read anything or see any street signs so he had to ask people to help—and not everybody has time for a poor beggar.

'When he got to the place where Jesus was due to pass by, Bartimaeus realised that there were

Reproduced with permission from *More Collective Worship Unwrapped* published by BRF 2010 (978 1 84101 664 1) **www.barnabasinschools.org.uk**

lots of other people there who wanted to meet Jesus, too. A great crowd, just like in that house in Capernaum, Ben—remember? Barty soon realised that he was at the back of the crowd, and he didn't know how close Jesus was, or even what direction he was facing. But he was absolutely determined not to miss his opportunity, so he took a deep breath and started shouting: "JESUS! PLEASE HELP ME!" People nearby told him to be quiet because he was embarrassing them but Bartimaeus wouldn't give up. He shouted even louder: "JESUS! SON OF DAVID! HELP ME!"

'Well, Jesus turned round and called Barty over. Then he touched his eyes and made him see again! "Just imagine, after all those years in the dark," Barty told me afterwards, "and the first thing I see is the lovely face of Jesus!" Bartimaeus loves reading now, but he's had to learn, just like you, Ben. And he's also learnt that no matter how hard it gets, we should never, ever give up!'

Reproduced with permission from *More Collective Worship Unwrapped* published by BRF 2010 (978 1 84101 664 1) www.barnabasinschools.org.uk

Mrs Bitsy and the little girl

STORYTELLING METHOD

Narrative with optional visual aids

Preparation

Take time to read the story through and practise retelling it in your own words.

Bible link

Mark 5:21–24, 35–43

Visual aids

❖ Articles associated with housework, shopping and so on
❖ A large and impressive clock
❖ To be really creative, you could bring a large honey cake and take the time to share it with a group of children after the assembly

Helpful hints: Be prepared to face some questions on death and bereavement. Young children are far less 'hung up' about this subject than some adults, so try to be honest about your own feelings. Take the opportunity to speak to a colleague or friend afterwards if you need to. There are several helpful books on talking about death and bereavement with children (see the Resources section on page 100). You'll also find a helpful assembly on this subject entitled 'Bubbles' in *Collective Worship Unwrapped*.

Main themes

Busyness and friendship

Further topics covered
Death and bereavement

Prayer

Dear Father God, thank you for all our friends and families. Help us not to be too busy to spend time with others, and comfort us when we feel sad. Amen

Songs

Kumbaya (JP)
Be still and know (JP)
God's not dead! (KS)

FOLLOW-UP

This is a good moment to have a circle time with a 'proxy teddy' or similar toy. Why was Mrs Bitsy so busy? What does it feel like when you have got too much to do? Do you think Jesus was ever too busy to spend time with people? How did Mrs Bitsy feel when her friend was made better? Why did she cry when she heard about Talitha?

This is the moment when you may or may not want to widen the discussion into the subject of death and bereavement. Be prepared to talk about pets as much as grandparents! If you know of particularly traumatic events connected with the school, such as the death of parents, teachers or even other children, be extra sensitive. .

You could end the follow-up time with a pleasant shared activity such as a game or some food—either healthy fruit or a big chocolate cake. Your call!

Mrs Bitsy was a bear—just a small brown furry teddy bear. But Mrs Bitsy was no ordinary teddy bear. Oh no! Mrs Bitsy was special. Mrs Bitsy loved everyone and everyone loved her. To you and me she looked like an ordinary bear, with a little red shawl and small round button eyes, but Mrs Bitsy had some amazing adventures. Would you like to hear one of them? You would? Well, listen carefully and I'll begin.

Mrs Bitsy was busy! Busy, busy, busy! There just didn't seem to be enough hours in the day today. Washing, ironing, gardening, sewing, cleaning—the list seemed endless. There was a cake to bake for poor Mrs Philipedes, who was poorly in bed, and then some errands to run for the synagogue leader, and she'd promised Ben a walk in the park together, and… oh! Where would she find the time?

Mrs Bitsy pulled on her shawl and hurried out of the door. It was early closing day at the market, but she might just have time to get her shopping. She scurried round the corner into Windey Street and ran straight into a huge crowd of people. They were all across the road—hundreds of people pressed shoulder to shoulder. Whatever were they doing? Mrs Bitsy could move quickly when she put her mind to it, so she sprang quickly up on to a rain barrel and from there to a high windowsill so that she could get a better look.

In the middle of the crowd she recognised a familiar figure. It was Jesus! He was smiling and shaking hands with everybody, talking to some of the older townspeople and picking up some of the younger children. Suddenly, there came a commotion at the back of the crowd. Someone was pushing through, crying out to Jesus.

'It's Mr Jairus!' shouted someone in the crowd. 'Make way for the synagogue leader!'

'Mr Jairus!' thought Mrs Bitsy. She'd promised to run some errands for him because his little daughter, Talitha, wasn't very well. How would she fit everything in? She was so busy!

Mrs Bitsy sits on her windowsill and watches the scene unfold…

Mr Jairus falls down at Jesus' feet. Whatever can be wrong? It's Talitha! She's very ill indeed! Mr Jairus thinks she may be dying! There's not a moment to lose. Jesus grabs Mr Jairus' hand and, with a reassuring smile, pulls him though the crowd and down the street, past Mrs Bitsy's watching place. 'Hmmm,' she thinks. 'Now Jesus is really busy, too!'

The crowd are still pressing tightly round Jesus. Mrs Bitsy can see that everyone seems to want to touch him. She smiles to herself. Jesus is so lovely! But now he's in a big hurry. He has to get to little Talitha quickly.

Suddenly Jesus stops and looks round. 'Who touched me?' he asks softly. Mrs Bitsy is amazed. Everyone is touching Jesus! Jesus waits and watches. Mr Jairus is getting very anxious. He knows how short the time is. Then, a shy, bent old woman reaches out to Jesus. 'It was me, Lord,' she says. 'I touched you. I have been ill for twelve years, but I knew if I could just touch you I would get better.' Mrs Bitsy recognises the woman straight away. It's poor Mrs Philipedes! Jesus hugs her at once. 'You are better,' he says to her. 'Your faith has made you well!'

Mrs Bitsy is so happy to see her friend well again, but she notices how upset Mr Jairus looks at the delay. Just then, one of Mr Jairus' servants pushes through the crowd. He has some very bad news indeed. Talitha has just died! It's too late.

Mr Jairus falls to the ground in shock and Mrs Bitsy's small round button eyes fill with tears. Everyone starts to cry but Jesus lifts Mr Jairus to his feet. 'Don't worry,' he says confidently. 'Just have faith.'

Nothing is going to distract Mrs Bitsy now. The market can wait. She follows Jesus and the crowd to Mr Jairus' house at the end of Windey Street. What will Jesus do?

At the house of Mr Jairus, Jesus leaves the crowd outside and goes to Talitha's room. Mrs Bitsy springs up on the windowsill and peers through the curtain. Mr Jairus and his wife are standing by Talitha's bed. The little girl is pale and still. Then

Reproduced with permission from *More Collective Worship Unwrapped* published by BRF 2010 (978 1 84101 664 1) www.barnabasinschools.org.uk

Jesus steps up, takes her hand and calls her. 'Talitha. Up you get!' Colour flows back into the little girl's face. She opens her eyes, takes a deep breath and jumps into Jesus' arms…

Later that day, Mrs Bitsy was back in her kitchen, having a cup of tea with Mrs Philipedes. Mrs Philipedes had baked Mrs Bitsy a honey cake and there was plenty to go round. 'I've learned an important lesson today, Dorcas,' said Mrs Bitsy to her old friend. 'You have to make time for the important things in life. It is possible to be too busy, you know. My shopping and housework can wait a bit. It's good to be with friends.'

Suddenly there came a knock at the door. 'That'll be Ben, come for our walk,' said Mrs Bitsy and, sure enough, there was her young neighbour. But he wasn't alone.

'I want you to meet my new friend, Mrs Bitsy,' said Ben, introducing a little girl only a few years older than him. 'Her name is Talitha. Can she come for a walk with us?'

'Come in, Talitha,' said Mrs Bitsy, pulling up two more chairs. 'Come in, Ben. There's always time for friends. Tell me, Talitha, do you like honey cake?'

Reproduced with permission from *More Collective Worship Unwrapped* published by BRF 2010 (978 1 84101 664 1) www.barnabasinschools.org.uk

Mrs Bitsy and the family feud

STORYTELLING METHOD

Narrative with optional visual aids

 Preparation

Take time to read the story through and practise retelling it in your own words.

 Bible link

John 21:1–4, 9–17

 Visual aids

You could tell the story straight without visual aids or you could set up a simple meal table with some food on it. If you are going to talk about the Jewish sabbath and the *seder* meal, you might also have some Jewish artefacts to hand.

Helpful hints: This is a good assembly for Passiontide, Easter and Passover.

 Main themes

Repentance, forgiveness and reconciliation

Further topics covered
Passover and hospitality

 Prayer

Father God, thank you so much that you forgive me even when I break my promises or I am unkind and selfish. Help me to be willing to say 'sorry', to own up to the wrong things I do and to forgive others as well. Amen

 Songs

I'm accepted, I'm forgiven (KS)
Come on and celebrate (KS)
The Spirit lives to set us free (KS)

FOLLOW-UP

This is another chance for circle time and/or sharing with the 'Mrs Bitsy' teddy or cuddly toy. How did the people feel around the table at the Barjonas' house? Mrs Barjonas? Ben? Mrs Bitsy? Simon, when he had let Jesus down? Has anyone ever let you down? How did you feel? How hard is it to say 'sorry' or to own up if you do something wrong?

With older children, this might lead into a discussion of Good Friday, Easter and Passover and possibly a project looking at the central values of Christianity and/or Judaism.

Mrs Bitsy was a bear—just a small brown furry teddy bear. But Mrs Bitsy was no ordinary teddy bear. Oh no! Mrs Bitsy was special. Mrs Bitsy loved everyone and everyone loved her. To you and me she looked like an ordinary bear, with a little red shawl and small round button eyes, but Mrs Bitsy had some amazing adventures. Would you like to hear one of them? You would? Well, listen carefully and I'll begin.

It was a dark and stormy night. Mrs Bitsy was round at the Barjonas' house for a special sabbath day supper. It was an extra-special occasion, too, because Mr Barjonas' brother Simon was visiting for the weekend.

'Baruch atah Adonai,' said everyone as Mrs Barjonas blessed the Shabbat candles and passed the bread to her brother-in-law.

As everyone began to eat the delicious food, Mrs Bitsy glanced across the table at young Benjamin. She couldn't believe how big he looked and how fast he was growing. There were just the six of them at the table now, including Ben's older brother Ethan, since both Rachel and Reuben were married and had homes of their own.

'And how is your beautiful daughter, Mrs Barjonas?' asked Mrs Bitsy. Mrs Barjonas said nothing but looked down at her plate.

'Mum and Rachel aren't talking any more, Mrs Bitsy,' said Ben, ignoring his mother's glares. 'I think they've had a row.'

'Now there's a pity, my dear,' said Mrs Bitsy. 'And she expecting that new baby so soon, as well.'

'Don't talk to me about new babies,' exclaimed Mrs Barjonas. 'That girl's not been the same since she set up house with that carpenter. She puts on too many airs and graces. Too good for the likes of us, she is!'

'Rebekah!' protested her husband from the other side of the table. '"That carpenter", as you put it, is our son-in-law and their new baby will be our grandchild. I do wish you would speak to her and put this silly argument behind you. Forgive and forget, I say!'

Mrs Barjonas grunted crossly and half rose from the table, but Simon gently touched her arm. 'My carpenter taught me a lot about forgiveness, Rebekah—the kind you never forget.'

'He means Jesus, the Great Rabbi, doesn't he, Mrs Bitsy?' whispered Ben as his mother slowly sat down and everyone turned to look at Simon. Mrs Bitsy nodded quietly.

'When Jesus was arrested in the garden that last night before he died,' Simon said, 'I made him a special promise, you know. I promised him I would look after all the others and, no matter what, I would never let him down. I promised him I would be there for him, but Jesus had told me that before the rooster crowed I would turn my back on him. And you know what? I did. Not once, but three times I said I didn't even know him. I was so ashamed! And when they beat him and told lies about him and spat on him and then finally killed him, I wasn't even there. When he needed me most, I ran away.'

'But the Great Rabbi didn't stay dead, did he, Uncle Simon?' blurted out Ben. 'He came alive again and lots of you saw him.'

'Yes, Ben, that's right,' went on Simon. 'One morning, a few days later, some of us were fishing—in this very lake where your dad does all his fishing—when Jesus met us on the beach. We had breakfast together. Everyone said it was like old times—except me. I couldn't look at him, you see. Even though he was alive and it was amazing, I couldn't forget how I'd let him down and broken my promise. Every time he tried to catch my eye, I looked away. Finally, he got up and came over to me and we walked along the beach together. And then, even after all he'd been through and after all my broken promises, he forgave me! He really did. Three times he said to me, "Simon Barjonas, do you love me?" I've never forgotten it.'

Mrs Barjonas looked up and a single tear rolled down her face. Mrs Bitsy laid a soft paw on her arm. 'It's not too late to invite two more to supper, is it?' she asked softly. 'Come on, I'll come with you.'

With that, Ben's mum and Mrs Bitsy left the table to take some forgiveness to their family and friends.

Key Stage One and Two assemblies

Ling and the emperor of China

STORYTELLING METHOD

To be told with dramatic narration and facial expression. This is a simple story told by heart or read from a book to encourage 'awe and wonder'.

 Preparation

Take time to read the story through and practise retelling it in your own words.

FOLLOW-UP

This story will provide an excellent opportunity to link the growth of seeds to the growth of character. You might like to start some projects on growing things—cress, beans, sunflowers and so on. Perhaps a visit to the school garden or a large community garden might be in order. How hard is it to do the right thing when everyone else is doing something different? What qualities made Ling so suitable to be the next emperor even though he was just a child? How could you 'grow' those qualities in your own life?

You might like to use some of the sentences below and 'unpack' some of them sensitively with your class.

If you plant dishonesty, you will reap distrust.
If you plant selfishness, you will reap loneliness.
If you plant envy, you will reap trouble.
If you plant bitterness, you will reap isolation.
If you plant greed, you will reap loss.
If you plant gossip, you will reap enemies.

If you plant honesty, you will reap trust.
If you plant goodness, you will reap friends.
If you plant hard work, you will reap success.
If you plant forgiveness, you will reap reconciliation.
If you plant patience, you will reap improvements.
If you plant faith, you will reap miracles.

 Bible link

Matthew 21:28–32

 Visual aids

❖ A decorative pot (although a plain one will do)
❖ A plum stone (or a screwed-up piece of paper) to simulate a seed

> Helpful hints: Make the story 'live' by the way you tell it. Emphasise especially the way Ling looks hopefully into the pot day by day, longing for his seed to grow.

 Main themes

Honesty and courage

Further topics covered
Patience and character

 Prayer

Dear God, help us to be just like Ling—brave, honest and true. Be close to us when others make fun of us and help us to stick up for what we know to be right. Amen

 Songs

Be bold, be strong (KS)
I want to be a tree that's bearing fruit (KS)
Have you got an appetite? (KS)

Once upon a time, far away and long ago in the great kingdom of China, the emperor was growing old. He knew it was time to choose his successor. But instead of choosing one of his assistants or one of his own family, he decided to do something different.

The great emperor called all the children and young people in the kingdom to his palace one day. He said, 'It is time for me to step down and choose the next emperor. I have decided to choose one of you.' The children were amazed, but the emperor continued, 'I am going to give each one of you a seed today—one very special seed. I want you to plant the seed, water it and take great care of it. Then you must come back here after one year from today with what you have grown from this one seed. I will then judge the plants that you bring and the one I choose will be the next emperor!'

A boy named Ling was there that day and he, like the others, received a seed. He went home and excitedly told his mother the story. She helped him find a pot and some planting soil and he planted the seed and watered it carefully. Every day he would water it and watch to see if it had grown. After about three weeks, some of the other children began to talk about their seeds and the plants that they were beginning to grow.

Ling kept checking his seed but nothing ever grew. Three weeks, four weeks, five weeks went by—still nothing. By now, others were talking about their plants, but Ling didn't have a plant and he felt as if he was a failure. Poor Ling! Six months went by, and still nothing in Ling's pot. He just knew he had killed his seed. Everyone else had trees and tall plants, but he had nothing. Ling didn't say anything to his friends, though. He just kept waiting for his seed to grow. 'Don't give up, Ling,' said his mother. 'The best things always take time to grow. Be patient, my son. Be brave!'

A year finally went by and it was time for all the children of the kingdom to bring their plants to the emperor for inspection. Ling told his mother that he wasn't going to take an empty pot. 'Be brave, Ling,' said his mother. 'Be honest, my son. Take your pot to the emperor.' Ling felt sick and afraid but he knew his mother was right. He took his empty pot to the emperor's palace. When Ling arrived, he was amazed at the variety of plants grown by the other children. They were beautiful and magnificent and glorious and in all different shapes and sizes. Ling put his empty pot on the floor and many of the others laughed at him. A few felt sorry for him and just said, 'Hey. Nice try!'

When the emperor arrived, he surveyed the room and greeted the young people. Ling just tried to hide at the back. 'What great plants, trees and flowers you have grown,' said the emperor. 'Today, one of you will be appointed the next emperor!' All of a sudden, the emperor spotted Ling at the back of the room with his empty pot. He ordered his guards to bring him to the front. Ling was terrified. 'The emperor knows I'm a failure! Maybe he will have me killed!' he thought.

When Ling got to the front, the emperor asked his name. 'My name is Ling,' he replied. Many of the other children were laughing and making fun of him. Suddenly, the emperor clapped his hands together and asked everyone to quieten down. He looked at Ling and then announced to the crowd, 'Behold your new emperor! His name is Ling!' Ling couldn't believe it. Ling couldn't even grow his seed. How could he be the new emperor? Then the emperor said, 'One year ago today, I gave everyone here a seed. I told you to take the seed, plant it, water it, take great care of it and bring it back to me today. But I gave you all boiled seeds which would not grow! All of you except Ling have brought me trees and plants and flowers. When you found that the seed would not grow, you substituted another seed for the one I gave you.

'Ling was the only one brave enough and honest enough to bring me a pot with my seed in it. Therefore, he is the one who will be the new emperor!'

Reproduced with permission from *More Collective Worship Unwrapped* published by BRF 2010 (978 1 84101 664 1) www.barnabasinschools.org.uk

The three trees

STORYTELLING METHOD

Dramatic narrative with (optional) visual aids

Preparation

Take time to read the story through and practise retelling it in your own words. Allow time, if necessary, to track down visual aids.

Bible link

Jeremiah 29:10–14

Visual aids (optional)

❖ Pictures of trees (audiovisual slides or posters)
❖ Small models of a manger, a boat and a cross, preferably made from wood
❖ The words 'What are your hopes and dreams?' left displayed on a screen or large sheet of card

---

Helpful hints: This is a simple story with a simple message. You could make it more interactive by having volunteers hold pictures of trees and/or the models of the manger, boat and cross. I have told this story using three green modelling balloons that become a manger, then a boat, then a cross. You could also use pipe cleaners, construction toys such as Lego or Duplo, or a creative PowerPoint presentation. Let your imagination run riot! This assembly will benefit from some classroom 'follow-up', particularly if you leave the children with a question about their hopes and dreams.

Main themes

Ambition and aspiration

Further topics covered

Patience, prayer, Christmas, Easter and the life of Jesus

Prayer

Dear God, you know our hopes and dreams. Give us patience and perseverance to see them fulfilled. Amen

Songs

See him lying on a bed of straw (KS)
Jesus bids us shine (JP)
This little light of mine (KS)
Jesus, we celebrate your victory (KS)

FOLLOW-UP

Try asking in a circle time what hopes and dreams the children might have. With younger (or more reserved) children, it might be helpful to pass a 'Mrs Bitsy' bear or other cuddly toy for the children to use as proxy. What did the trees want to become? What did they actually become? What was hardest for the trees to accept? How do we handle disappointment? How easy is it to forget our dreams when we have to wait a long time? What helps dreams come true?

'Show and Tell' has a bit of a 'cheesy' reputation but it might be worth asking the children to bring something to school that has been made from a tree and, if they wish, to talk to the rest of the class about it.

Once there were three trees on a hill in the woods. They were discussing their hopes and dreams when the first tree said, 'Some day I hope to be a treasure chest. I could be filled with gold, silver and precious gems. I could be decorated with intricate carving and everyone would see my beauty.'

Then the second tree said, 'Some day I will be a mighty ship. I will take kings and queens across the waters and sail to the corners of the world. Everyone will feel safe in me because of the strength of my great hull.'

Finally, the third tree said, 'I want to grow to be the tallest and straightest tree in the forest. People will see me on top of the hill and look up to my branches, and think of the heavens and God and how close to them I am reaching. I will be the greatest tree of all time and people will always remember me.'

After a few years of hoping that their dreams would come true, the trees were found by a group of wood cutters. When one came to the first tree, he said, 'This looks like a strong tree. I think I should be able to sell the wood to a carpenter,' and he began cutting it down. The tree was happy because he knew that the carpenter would make him into a beautiful treasure chest.

At the second tree, the wood cutter said, 'This looks like a strong tree. I should be able to sell it to the shipyard.' The second tree was happy because she knew she was on her way to becoming a mighty ship.

When the wood cutters came to the third tree, he was frightened because he knew that if he was cut down, his dream would not come true. One of the wood cutters said, 'I don't need anything special from my tree. I'll take this one,' and cut it down.

When the first tree arrived at the carpenters, he was made into a feed box for animals. He was then placed in a barn and filled with hay. This was not at all what he had hoped for.

The second tree was cut and made into a small fishing boat. Her dreams of being a mighty ship and carrying kings had come to an end.

The third tree was cut into large pieces and left alone in the dark.

The years went by and, after a while, the trees forgot about their hopes and dreams.

Then, one day, a man and woman came to the barn where the first tree had been put, made into a feed box. The woman was expecting a baby and the time had come for her to give birth. When the baby was born, his mother placed him in the hay in the feed box. The man wished that he could have made a crib for the baby, but this manger would have to do. The tree could feel the importance of this event and somehow realised that he was holding the greatest treasure of all time.

Years later, a group of men got into the fishing boat made from the second tree. One of them was tired and fell asleep. While they were out on the water, a great storm arose, and the tree didn't think she was strong enough to keep the men safe. The men woke their sleeping friend, he stood up and said 'Peace'… and the storm stopped. The tree realised that she had carried the King of all kings in her hull.

Finally, someone came to fetch the third tree. He was carried through the streets by a man who was mocked by the people all around. When they came to a halt, the man was nailed to the tree and raised in the air to die at the top of a hill. When Sunday came, the tree began to realise that he was strong enough to stand at the top of the hill and be as close to God as possible, because of the man who had been nailed upon him. He had indeed become the greatest 'tree' of all time and was remembered across the world.

Despite everything, the hopes and dreams of all three trees had been realised.

The moral of this story is that when things don't seem to be going our way, we can always know that God has a plan for us. If we place our trust in him, he will give us great gifts. Each of the trees got what they wanted—just not in the way they had imagined. We don't always know what God's plans are for us. We only know that his ways are not our ways, but his ways are always best.

Reproduced with permission from *More Collective Worship Unwrapped* published by BRF 2010 (978 1 84101 664 1) www.barnabasinschools.org.uk

The three questions

This assembly is based on another of Leo Tolstoy's short stories (like 'Arthur and the magic fish' in *Collective Worship Unwrapped*).

STORYTELLING METHOD

Dramatic narrative with some pupil interaction

 Preparation

Take time to read the story through and practise retelling it in your own words. Allow a little extra time if you require visual aids.

 Bible link

Philippians 2:1–5

FOLLOW-UP

This is a good opportunity for a wide-ranging discussion on what makes life important. Ask the children if they have any other suggestions about what is the most important time, the most important person and the most important thing to do. Why do you think the emperor thought these questions were so important? How did the hermit show the emperor the answer to his questions even though he said very little? Why do you think it is so difficult to forgive other people? Is it ever right to pay someone back if they hurt us?

Ask the children to come back to the next class sharing time with a simple idea to change the world. In the meantime, you could check out the movie *Pay it Forward*.

 Visual aids

- ❖ A simple crown made from card
- ❖ A kingly cloak
- ❖ A battered hat or cap and scarf
- ❖ A shovel

> **Helpful hints:** Like all good stories, this needs little more than to be told well. I've found that this story captivates all ages. The visual aids help a little, but don't rely on them. Use voice characterisation if you want to, but keep it simple. There is little humour but a lot of drama and the oft-repeated questions should further engage the children.

 Main themes

Life values, relationships and making a difference

Further topics covered
Forgiveness and kindness

 Prayer

Dear God, thank you for our friends and family. Help us to remember that the most important time is right now and the most important person is the one we are with. Help us to try to make a difference in your world by helping them. Thank you, God. Amen

 Songs

Spirit of the living God (JP)
I'm accepted, I'm forgiven (KS)
Give me oil in my lamp (KS)

Once upon a time, it occurred to a certain emperor that if he only knew the answers to three questions, he would never stray in any matter. Here are the three questions. Perhaps you'd like to say them after me.

'What is the most important time? Who are the most important people? What is the most important thing to do?'

Think carefully now. These are important questions. What do you think?

Invite some contributions from the floor.

Hmmm. Those are all good suggestions. Let's get back to the story and see if any of them are right.

The emperor issued a decree throughout his kingdom, announcing that whoever could answer the questions would receive a great reward. Many who read the decree made their way to the palace at once, each person with a different answer. What were the questions again?

'What is the most important time? Who are the most important people? What is the most important thing to do?'

In reply to the first question, one person advised the emperor to make up a thorough time schedule, dedicating every hour, day, month and year to certain tasks, and then follow the schedule to the letter. Only then could he hope to carry out every task at the right time.

Another person replied that it was impossible to plan in advance and that the emperor should put all vain amusements aside and remain attentive to everything in order to know what to do at what time.

Someone else insisted that, by himself, the emperor could never hope to have all the foresight and competence necessary to decide when to do each and every task. What he really needed was to set up a Council of the Wise and act according to their advice.

Someone else said that certain matters required an immediate decision and could not wait for consultation. If he wanted to know in advance what was going to happen, he should consult magicians and soothsayers.

The responses to the second question also differed greatly.

One person said that the emperor needed to place all his trust in administrators, another urged reliance on priests and monks, while others recommended physicians. Still others put their faith in warriors.

The third question drew a similar variety of answers. Some said that science was the most important pursuit. Others insisted on religion. Yet others claimed that the most important thing was military skill.

The emperor was not pleased with any of the answers, and no reward was given. Still he pondered the questions…

(Say together) 'What is the most important time? Who are the most important people? What is the most important thing to do?'

After several nights of reflection, the emperor resolved to visit a hermit who lived up on the mountain and was said to be an enlightened man. The emperor wished to find the hermit to ask him the three questions. However, he knew that the hermit never left the mountain and was known to receive only the poorest of people, refusing to have anything to do with persons of wealth or power. So the emperor disguised himself as a simple peasant and ordered his attendants to wait for him at the foot of the mountain while he climbed the slope alone to seek the hermit.

Reaching the holy man's dwelling place, the emperor found the hermit digging a garden in front of his hut. When the hermit saw the stranger, he nodded his head in greeting and continued to dig. The labour was obviously hard on him. He was an old man, and each time he thrust his spade into the ground to turn the earth, he breathed heavily.

The emperor approached him and said, 'I have come here to ask your help with three questions:

(Say together) 'What is the most important time?

Reproduced with permission from *More Collective Worship Unwrapped* published by BRF 2010 (978 1 84101 664 1) www.barnabasinschools.org.uk

Who are the most important people? What is the most important thing to do?'

The hermit listened attentively but only patted the emperor on the shoulder and continued digging. The emperor said, 'You must be tired. Here, let me give you a hand with that.' The hermit thanked him, handed the emperor the spade, and then sat down on the ground to rest.

After he had dug two rows, the emperor stopped and turned to the hermit and repeated his three questions:

(Say together) 'What is the most important time? Who are the most important people? What is the most important thing to do?'

The hermit still did not answer, but instead stood up, pointed to the spade and said, 'Why don't you rest now? I can take over again.' But the emperor continued to dig. One hour passed, then two. Finally the sun began to set behind the mountain. The emperor put down the spade and said to the hermit, 'I came here to ask if you could answer my three questions. But if you can't give me any answer, please let me know so that I can get on my way home.'

The hermit lifted his head and asked the emperor, 'Do you hear someone running over there?' The emperor turned his head. They both saw a man with a long white beard emerge from the woods. He ran wildly, pressing his hands against a bleeding wound in his stomach. The man ran toward the emperor before falling to the ground, where he lay unconscious. Opening the man's clothing, the emperor and hermit saw that he had received a deep gash. The emperor cleaned the wound thoroughly and then used his own shirt to bandage it, but the blood completely soaked the bandage within minutes. He rinsed the shirt out and bandaged the wound again, and continued to do so until the flow of blood had stopped.

At last the wounded man regained consciousness and asked for a drink of water. The emperor ran down to the stream and brought back a jug of fresh water. Meanwhile, the sun had disappeared and the night air had begun to turn cold. The hermit gave the emperor a hand in carrying the man into the hut, where they laid him down on the hermit's bed. The man closed his eyes and lay quietly. The emperor was worn out from the long day of climbing the mountain and digging the garden, and he still had no answer to his three questions:

(Say together) 'What is the most important time? Who are the most important people? What is the most important thing to do?'

Leaning against the doorway, the emperor fell asleep. When he woke, the sun had already risen over the mountain. For a moment he couldn't remember where he was and what he had come there for. He looked over to the bed and saw the wounded man also looking around him in confusion. When the man saw the emperor, he stared at him intently and then said in a faint whisper, 'Please forgive me.'

'But what have you done, that I should forgive you?' the emperor asked.

'You do not know me, your majesty, but I know you. I was your sworn enemy, and I had vowed to take vengeance on you, for during the last war you killed my brother and seized my property. When I learned that you were coming alone to the mountain to meet the hermit, I resolved to surprise you on your way back, to kill you. After waiting a long time, there was still no sign of you, so I left my ambush in order to seek you out. But instead of finding you, I came across your attendants, who recognised me and gave me this wound. Luckily, I escaped and ran here. If I hadn't met you, I would surely be dead by now. I had intended to kill you but instead you saved my life! I am ashamed and grateful beyond words. If I live, I vow to be your servant as long as I live, and I will bid my children and grandchildren to do the same. Please grant me your forgiveness.'

The emperor was overjoyed to see that he was so easily reconciled with a former enemy. He not only forgave the man, but promised to return all the property he had seized and to send his own doctor and servants to wait on the man until he was completely healed. After ordering his attendants to

Reproduced with permission from *More Collective Worship Unwrapped* published by BRF 2010 (978 1 84101 664 1) www.barnabasinschools.org.uk

take the man home, the emperor went in to see the hermit. Before returning to the palace, the emperor wanted to repeat his three questions one last time. He found the hermit sowing seeds in the earth they had dug the day before. He asked one last time:

(Say together) 'What is the most important time? Who are the most important people? What is the most important thing to do?'

The hermit stood up and looked at the emperor. 'But your questions have already been answered.'

'How's that?' the emperor asked, puzzled.

'Yesterday, if you had not taken pity on my age and given me a hand with digging these beds, you would have been attacked by that man on your way home. Then you would have deeply regretted not staying with me. Therefore the most important time was the time you were digging in the beds, the most important person was myself, and the most important thing to do was to help me. Later, when the wounded man ran up here, the most important time was the time you spent dressing his wound, for if you had not cared for him he would have died and you would have lost the chance to be reconciled with him. Likewise, he was the most important person, and the most important thing to do was taking care of his wound.

'Remember that there is only one important time, and that is now. The present moment is the only time over which we have control. The most important person is always the person you are with, who is right before you, for who knows if you will have dealings with any other person in the future. The most important thing to do is making that person, the one standing at your side, happy, for that alone is the pursuit of life.'

(Ask and wait for the answers) What is the most important time? 'Now.'

Who are the most important people? 'The people you are with.'

What is the most important thing to do? 'Help them and try to make them happy.'

Reproduced with permission from *More Collective Worship Unwrapped* published by BRF 2010 (978 1 84101 664 1) www.barnabasinschools.org.uk

The chocolate prodigal

I couldn't really blame this assembly on anyone other than myself. The puns are just too bad! (The chocolate is good, though.) This is an unusual presentation of the story of the lost son—one of Jesus' better-known stories. The visual aids will elicit a lot of excitement so the whole assembly needs to be handled carefully if a sense of awe and wonder is to be maintained. The chocolate version is based on an item called 'Sweet story' originally published by ROOTS for Churches* in 2004. My story would have used a greater variety of confectionery but I was restricted by copyright considerations. You, on the other hand, are limited only by your imagination and sense of humour!

* *ROOTS for Churches* produce weekly lectionary-based worship and learning resources. Find out more at www.rootsontheweb.com.

STORYTELLING METHOD

Slightly 'off the wall' with attractive visual aids and lots of interaction from the children (and quite possibly, the teachers, too!)

Preparation

Take time to read the story through and practise retelling it in your own words.

Bible link

Luke 15:11–32

Visual aids

The branded chocolates mentioned in the story and a board to attach them to. (If real chocolate causes concern, just do the 'calorie-free' version and show pictures of the chocolate bars.)

Helpful hints: This is an assembly that needs to be delivered very carefully. If you do decide to present it with real chocolate, you will need the head teacher's agreement beforehand on the best way to do it. It is unlikely to be a good idea to allow the children to consume the chocolate during the assembly. It might be best to keep it until break or the end of school. You will also need to be aware of children who have allergies or whose parents would not approve of chocolate. Having the 'Heroes' at the end means that you could share them out with the winning class or even the whole school. Broadly speaking, there needs to be a balance between proper discipline and good clean fun! If you cannot get all the brands of chocolate indicated, either change the words or make up your own alternatives using brands of sweets and chocolates that you can obtain. Or why not revamp the whole thing and try lots of healthy fruit? Just use your imagination!

Main themes

Repentance and forgiveness

Further topics covered

Sharing, jealousy and responsibility

Prayer

Dear God, help me to be grateful for all I have and to be willing to admit when I am wrong. Help me not to be jealous when others seem to have more than me. Thank you, God. Amen

Songs

Have you got an appetite? (KS)
Jehoveh Jireh, God will provide (KS)
Give thanks with a grateful heart (KS)

FOLLOW-UP

This is an opportunity for a discussion on the interesting subject of forgiveness. How does it feel when someone lets you down? Has that ever happened to you? How do you feel if the person is a close friend or family member? How do you think the father felt in the story? Why did the younger brother spend all his father's inheritance? How much courage does it take to admit you are wrong and say sorry? How did the younger son feel when his father forgave him? Why was the older brother so upset with the father?

Christians believe this story teaches us some important lessons about God. What do you think these might be?

Here's a well-known story from the Bible that Jesus told to show his friends what God is like. I've hidden some sweets in the story so you'll need to listen very carefully. If you spot one, don't shout out. Just put your hand up and, if you're asked, you can come and pick the sweet from the board. (Another member of staff should do the picking out. Children might be encouraged to give the chocolate to their teacher for later.)

Once upon a time there was a man who had two sons. Frederick, the older son, was hard-working and conscientious but Simon, the younger son, was a bit of a FLAKE. One day, Simon said to his father, 'Hey, Dad—I could do with a BOOST to my finances. Give me my share of the family inheritance now.' Then, jumping aboard the first DOUBLE DECKER into town, he took some TIME OUT with his friends, visiting STAR BARs and other hangouts of the rich and famous.

One day, it came to the CRUNCHIE ('crunch; he', pay attention!) realised all his money was gone and all he had in his pocket were a few BUTTONS. No more TURKISH DELIGHT for him; it was time to look for work!

The only job he managed to get was working for a famous Michelin four-star patisserie chef with the unlikely name of Signor FERRERO ROCHER. Although he would like to have worked in the DAIRY MILKing cows, he ended up looking after pigs with their noses all turned up and their tails all CURLY WURLY. At night he would DREAM of home and hoped his father might not reFUSE to take him back.

Finally he decided not to FUDGE the issue any longer and he said to himself, 'I will go to my father, admit that I was wrong and ask his forgiveness.' So he ROSES (rose, his) mind made up, and set off home to say sorry to his dad. While he was still some way off, his father saw him and ran to greet his son. He was so happy he did a TWIRL and hugged his boy. Then he called for a party and all the family rejoiced—all apart from the older brother, who felt bitter and TWISTED.

'All this time with you, Father, and not a WISPA of encouragement,' he said. 'You didn't even give me as much as a PICNIC. Why should this no-good son of yours deserve anything?'

'FREDDO,' said his father, 'you are always with me and all I have is yours. But your brother was lost and now is found. It's time for a HEROES' welcome!'

ADAPTED FROM A STORY PUBLISHED BY
ROOTS FOR CHURCHES LTD

Reproduced with permission from *More Collective Worship Unwrapped* published by BRF 2010 (978 1 84101 664 1) www.barnabasinschools.org.uk

The faithful dog

The following story was given to me by Alan Clark, a former head teacher and the Foreword writer for *Collective Worship Unwrapped*. He says it never failed to evoke 'awe and wonder' in his pupils and draw a tear from his own eye. The story is taken from *101 School Assembly Stories Book 1* by Frank Carr (Foulsham, 1973). I've added a few embellishments of my own, but the story should be told pretty much as it was originally written.

STORYTELLING METHOD

A simple tale, told with sincerity

Preparation

Take time to read the story through and practise retelling it in your own words. Also allow time to obtain visual aids, if used.

Bible link

Psalm 89:1–8

Visual aids

* ❖ A large book to read from
* ❖ A suitable picture of a man and a dog
* ❖ To add some further authenticity, you could dress up either as a soldier or as an Australian farmer (jacket, hat with corks and so on)

Helpful hints: Children, especially younger ones, are very sensitive so be prepared for some emotional reactions and deal with them appropriately through the quiet reflective time that follows.

Main themes

Loyalty and friendship; trust and faithfulness; awe and wonder

Further topics covered

Pets, war, grief and loss

Prayer

Dear God, thank you for the faithfulness and love that Tom and Scruff showed to each other. Thank you for the faithfulness and love of all our friends and family. Thank you for being so faithful and loving to us. Help us to be faithful and loving too. Amen

Songs

Kumbaya (JP)
Be still and know (JP)
Give thanks with a grateful heart (KS)

FOLLOW-UP

Who was bravest in the story? Tom for going off to war, or Scruff for waiting patiently for so long? Does anyone know of a faithful pet like Scruff? What does your pet do to show loyalty? What things do we need to do to show loyalty and faithfulness? How do we feel when someone lets us down? How can we all be more loyal and dependable?

Describe the most loyal and dependable person you know (real or imaginary). What makes them so special? You could compile a scrapbook of faithful friends and include pets, family and friends and even famous or special 'heroes'.

Begin by talking a little about the Psalms. You could put Psalm 89:1–8 on the screen. Explain that psalms are like songs that tell us what God is like, and this one talks about his faithfulness. Ask for a definition of faithfulness or if anyone has ever experienced it. Now briefly introduce the story and perhaps take the opportunity to put on your hat and pick up your 'story book'.

Tom lived in what the Australians call the outback, the great open spaces in which the neighbouring farm may be 50 miles away. He had no playmates on the small sheep-farm that his parents ran so they bought him a fluffy puppy to keep him company. Tom was delighted. Every day he would take Scruff out to the nearby hills and they would roll and play, hunt rabbits and chase kangaroos until the sun dipped behind the hills.

The years passed. Tom was 18 and Scruff was a full-grown dog when war broke out in 1939. Tom decided that he should join the army and fight in the war. So one day he put on his knapsack and said goodbye to his parents. They stood outside the farm, close to tears, as the boy set off. Scruff, who had always gone everywhere with Tom, trotted along at his heels. Tom stopped and said, 'Not this time, old fellow,' and shooed the dog back to his mum and dad. They watched as Tom disappeared over the brow of the hill, and then they went indoors sadly.

Next day, Tom's mum and dad found Scruff lying on the road at noon, his eyes fixed on the top of the hill. He was waiting for his master's return. He stayed there for hours and finally came indoors, his tail drooping with disappointment. He did the same thing the next day and the next, and the pattern repeated itself from then on.

Soon they received a cheerful letter from Tom. He was in Europe, he told them, and they must not worry about him. But of course they did. The newspapers were full of stories about fierce fighting in France. Tom's letters became rarer as he found himself in the battle area. Then, one dreadful day, a letter came from the Australian government telling them that Tom was 'missing, believed killed'.

Tom's mum and dad were shattered. Tom was their only child, their whole family. Their lives seemed nothing without him. They didn't care about anything any more. Only Scruff seemed not to be affected. He continued to lie in the road at midday, staring at the top of the hill where his master had disappeared so long ago.

Nobody was surprised when Tom's father grew ill and died. 'He didn't want to live,' they said. And when, not long after, his mother passed away, they simply shook their heads. Two neighbours took Scruff to live at their farm 20 miles away. Next morning he was gone. They found him at noon, at his post outside the boarded-up farm, gazing patiently up the road. They took him back to their home. He ran away again. They fetched him back. He ran away. So they gave up.

Scruff then became a wild dog, living in the bush and eating what he could kill by hunting. His coat grew dirty and his body thin, but every day he took up his position in the road when the sun was hottest, and waited. Hours later he would rise and lope off sadly back into the bush. Now and then, a stranger would come down the dirt road. Scruff would rise, ears pricked, and watch until his failing eyesight told him it was not Tom. Then he would slink off once again.

A year passed. Scruff was slower now and there was plenty of grey fur around his mouth. He could not run so quickly and food was scarce. His bones could be clearly seen through his filthy coat.

One day he took up his post on the road, his muzzle resting on the ground, his tired old eyes fixed on the hill. A figure came over the crest. Scruff raised his head but did not move. The stranger approached. Something about the swing of his arms, the set of his shoulders, brought the dog to his feet, his eyes straining to see more clearly. Then he moved forward, at first slowly, then more quickly, and finally he broke into a run and flung himself into Tom's arms. The soldier stood there for a long time, hugging the old dog, tears running down his cheeks and on to Scruff's filthy coat. Then Tom took the boards off the windows of the farm and they went inside to start their lives again. The dog's loyalty and affection were finally rewarded.

This would be an appropriate time to move into a period of quiet reflection. Light a candle and/ or play some suitable music. Say a few guiding words and encourage the children to maintain some silence for thinking. If suitable, you could use prayers similar to the one provided.

Honky the Donkey's busy day

This story follows up the assembly from *Collective Worship Unwrapped* based on the story of the good Samaritan, and reacquaints the children with Henry, Sam and Honky the Donkey.

STORYTELLING METHOD

Narrative with a tag line

 Preparation

Take time to read the story through and practise retelling it in your own words. Allow time to find visual aids, if used.

Bible link

John 12:12–21

 FOLLOW-UP

This story once more states the inherent value in all of us and the need to affirm that we are all special. (Think Kevin Costner in *Field of Dreams*.) The following questions might be useful. Have you ever had a dream of what you might become? Would you like to share it? What do you think of the dreams expressed on television programmes such as *X Factor*? Is it good to have something like that to believe in? What can we do to make our dream become a reality? How do you respond when others tell you their dreams? What was unique and special about Honky the Donkey? What do you think is unique and special about you?

Take some time to affirm each other and engage in some exercises that will build self-esteem.

 Visual aids

A donkey! This could be a balloon donkey, a toy donkey or a picture of Honky the Donkey photocopied from page 95 or downloaded from the website: www.barnabasinschools.org.uk/morecollectiveworship.

> Helpful hints: You could start by making a balloon donkey and asking children to guess what it might be, or produce a donkey from a bag or have Honky gradually appear on a screen.

 Main themes

Self-esteem and being special

Further topics covered
Personal significance and realising dreams; Palm Sunday and Holy Week

 Prayer

Lord God, help us to realise our dreams and never give up believing that they can come true. Thank you for believing in us and making all of us the special, unique people that we are. Amen

 Songs

Lord, we come to worship you (SFK)
Oh, oh, oh, how good is the Lord! (KS)
Lord of the dance (JP)
Give me oil in my lamp (KS)

You may remember the exciting story of Honky the Donkey and the adventure he had with Henry *(wait for the 'Yo, Henry!' or explain how it worked in the previous story)*. This time, since Henry *(Yo, Henry!)* doesn't appear in this story *(ohhhh)*… well, he was just too busy, I'm afraid… we're going to have to listen out for Honky the Donkey and make two thumbs up every time we hear his name and say 'Go, Honky!'

Now Honky the Donkey *(Go, Honky!)* never forgot his exciting adventure with Henry *(Yo, Henry!)* (Hey! I said he wasn't in this story!) and the robbers and how important it made him feel. Everyone had stroked him at McDonalds and someone had even given him a McCreamEgg to eat all to himself. So many children wanted to ride on his back in the donkey park outside that he went 'Heee haaaw! Heee haaaw!' until he nearly became a little hoarse(!)

Optional beginning for those who haven't encountered Honky before

Once … upon… a… time… there… was… a little grey donkey. His name was Honky the Donkey and he always dreamed of having adventures. Whenever you hear his name in the story, just make two thumbs up and say 'Go, Honky!' OK? Let's have a quick practice: 'Honky the Donkey!' *(Go, Honky!)* Honky the Donkey *(Go, Honky!)* had had one adventure long ago when he'd helped a man called Henry who was attacked by robbers…

But all that was forgotten now and Honky the Donkey *(Go, Honky!)* was back to his chores, carrying bundles to market or Sam, his owner, to the nearby town. But most of the time Honky the Donkey *(Go, Honky!)* just stood in the field and chewed the grass. 'Why can't something exciting happen to me?' he thought to himself as he munched on a thistle. 'Like when Sam and I

rescued Henry *(Yo, Henry!)* (I thought I'd said he wasn't in this story!) from the big hole.'

Honky the Donkey *(Go, Honky!)* dreamed of having exciting adventures, sailing with pirates or exploring distant lands. He dreamed of winning races, climbing mountains and even working behind the counter at McDonalds. He thought about learning to speak like a human being—as one of his ancestors had done, so it is told. I guess he would even have dreamed of water-skiing and hang-gliding if they had been invented!

Honky the Donkey *(Go, Honky!)* was bored. Even eating Sam's neighbours' washing was losing its appeal and he'd lost his appetite for string vests. If only Honky *(Go, Honky!)* could be famous, he thought to himself, then people would never forget him or think of him as just a silly and annoying donkey. So Honky *(Go, Honky!)* stayed in the field with his dreams and his memories. Until…

One day, Sam the Samaritan, the donkey's owner, took Honky *(Go, Honky!)* to the big city. They had no exciting adventures on the way. They saw no robbers and no big holes in the ground. They didn't even stop at McDonalds *(ohhhh)* and they saw no sign of anyone called Henry… (uh… don't say it!) When Sam reached the big city, he left Honky *(Go, Honky!)* tied up outside a house while he went off to do what he had come for.

'Here we go again,' thought the donkey to himself, 'all on my own again. Forgotten, as usual. If only I could be a tall white horse with a golden bit and bridle, then people would notice me! Imagine me stamping the ground and snorting through my nostrils. Heee haaaw!' Hmmm.

But nobody noticed the little grey donkey. Until…

Someone he didn't recognise came along and untied him. 'The Master needs you,' they said and led him away. After a short while, that person brought the donkey to a man who got on to Honky's *(Go, Honky!)* back. Honky *(Go, Honky!)* realised somehow that this was someone very special indeed.

Reproduced with permission from *More Collective Worship Unwrapped* published by BRF 2010 (978 1 84101 664 1) www.barnabasinschools.org.uk

The donkey was led down the street and suddenly they were surrounded by crowds and crowds of people—men, women and children—all shouting and laughing and cheering. Honky *(Go, Honky!)* could hear what some of them were shouting. 'Hooray! God bless the one who comes in the name of the Lord! God bless the King of Israel!'

'A king? … A king!' thought the donkey. 'I'm carrying a king! I can hardly believe it!' And a great big donkey smile came over his donkey face.

Later that day, when he had been taken back to the place where he'd been left, Honky the Donkey *(Go, Honky!)* could hardly believe he had had such a busy and exciting day. Had it all been only a dream?

But as he stood in his field next morning and looked at his reflection in his drinking trough, Honky *(Go, Honky!)* saw that the coat on his back was marked with a special new sign—a long dark cross. He realised then that he had carried the King of all kings on his back and that his story would never be forgotten.

Reproduced with permission from *More Collective Worship Unwrapped* published by BRF 2010 (978 1 84101 664 1) **www.barnabasinschools.org.uk**

Key Stage Two
assemblies

Seeing is believing... or is it?

This can be a quite short assembly and is ideal for Easter time, covering, as it does, the subject of Christian faith. It relies almost entirely upon your performance of an amazing and unlikely stunt, so be prepared!

STORYTELLING METHOD

Conveying a message through an entertaining stunt

Preparation

Very little preparation time is required if you are imaginative, more so if you need to prepare some surprising stunts.

Bible link

John 20:19–20, 24–31

Visual aids

❖ You (or a talented friend) plus anything you have chosen with which to 'surprise' the children

---

Helpful hints: This assembly relies heavily on the surprise element. The first time I did it, I arrived with a small bunch of daffodils. I then greeted the school in Welsh, ate the daffodils,* cartwheeled in full clerical garb across the front of the hall and kissed the head teacher. You might not want to go quite that far! The important thing is that you (or an accomplice) does something surprising. It could be a magic trick or even escapology (see 'The man who wasn't there' or 'Peter the escape artist' in *Collective Worship Unwrapped*). However, be sure to remind the children not to copy you, as you are a 'professional'. You may feel it inappropriate to do something outrageous in front of the children, especially if you have to teach them immediately afterwards. Being a clown as well as a vicar, I can get away with quite a lot, but if you are uncomfortable with this scenario, hire a Christian entertainer.

If you can't do a stunt or hire an entertainer, try displaying some optical illusions on a screen. There are some great ones on www.kids.niehs.nih.gov/illusion/illusions.htm and a brief trawl of the internet should turn up quite a few more. Be creative! After your stunt and/or presentation, proceed with the story on page 68.

* It is quite safe to eat daffodils as long as they are the right variety and you only eat the heads, not the stems.

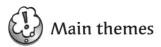 Main themes

Faith and belief

Further topics covered
Easter

 Prayer

Dear God, help us to realise that we cannot see or touch everything we believe in. Thank you for the values and beliefs that guide our lives and give us the faith to put our trust in you. Amen

 Songs

God's not dead! (KS)
Jesus, we celebrate your victory (KS)
This is the day (JP)

FOLLOW-UP

A discussion of Christian faith and belief would be quite appropriate here. Be sensitive to different belief and value systems and be aware of children from homes with strong religious views. If there has been an element of conjuring in the assembly, you might like to discuss the difference between magic and miracles. You could even teach the class a simple trick. For example, hold up the first finger of each hand, then bang your hands together three or four times and on the last time drop the finger of one hand and raise the second finger on the other hand. It's really silly but it appears as if one finger has jumped across.

Ask children to describe amazing things that they have seen, which made them doubt the evidence of their own eyes. Is seeing believing? Does what we believe in have to be touchable? Ask for examples of things we believe in that cannot be seen. You could finish with a project looking at what people believe in various world faiths.

Now if you go home tonight and tell your parents that the person taking your assembly… *(recap your stunt)* they'll say, 'I don't believe you!' You might even have thought that yourselves. You might be saying, 'I've seen it but I can't believe it!'

That happened a lot with Jesus' friends, you know, because Jesus did so many amazing things, they could hardly believe their eyes. One of the most amazing was coming back to life after he had died. One of his friends wouldn't believe it unless he saw the evidence with his own eyes. When he did, Jesus told him that in future the people who would be really blessed were those who didn't see and yet believed.

It's true that you can't believe everything you see—but you can't see everything you believe, either!

End the assembly with a time of reflection, using candles and/or suitable music and a short prayer if that is appropriate.

The Two Johns

The Two Johns are my own invention, shamelessly based on 'The Two Rons', popularised by comedians Hale and Pace. I used to perform the sketches in DJs and shades with a friend who is 6' 9". Since I am 5' 3", we make an interesting pair! The dialogues work well because they are short, sharp and aggressive (in a humorous way) and convey a clear Christian message. Years later I still bump into ex-pupils who remember 'The Two Johns'.

The sketches are best played 'deadpan' with a broad East End or South Essex accent. John One is the boss and John Two is the stooge, thick as two short planks but with a heart of gold. They act in a very intimidating way but all the violence and aggression is by implication only. If your abilities don't run to this kind of acting, get a couple of likely characters to act the sketch and then follow it with your own two-minute epilogue. If the two Johns can sustain the act, all these sketches can be followed up with classwork where pupils interview the Johns, still in character.

The Two Johns

Remembrance Day

STORYTELLING METHOD

Dramatic and humorous dialogue

 Preparation

Take time to read through the script and allow for a short rehearsal. Also, allow time to prepare the costumes or to make contact with people to play the characters.

 Bible link

Joshua 4:1–9

 Visual aids

❖ Two confident and imaginative actors dressed in DJs and shades
❖ A big Bible
❖ A large and impressive-looking imitation rocket-type firework
❖ A bucket of stones

> Helpful hints: Try to get your two Johns to stay 'in character' from the moment they enter the school hall to the moment they leave. They are supposed to appear intimidating and scary (in a humorous way). Most of the time, when they are not performing, they can just stand at the side and look menacing.

 Main themes

Remembrance Day and Bonfire night

Further topics covered
Responsibility; conflict and war

 Prayer

Dear Lord, help us to remember the things that matter. Be close to all who suffer as a result of war, and bring peace to the nations of the earth. Amen

 Songs

The remember song (see page 20)
We're marching along (KS)
Make me a channel of your peace (JP)

FOLLOW-UP

This is an excellent opportunity for the two Johns to chair a discussion on the subject of war and conflict. This topic will also link up with curriculum areas of 20th-century history in the discussion of World Wars I and II. On a lighter note, there could also be some memory games. There are a number of versions of these on the Internet. Try www.faculty.washington.edu/chudler/chmemory.html.

You could also take a look at the passage from Joshua 4 and discuss the place of 'remembering stones'. Can you think of any other important stones mentioned in the Bible? What about gravestones and monuments? What is the significance of places such as Mount Rushmore, Uluru (Ayers Rock), Nelson's Column or the Obelisk? (Add your own local statues and monuments.) What do you think of when you see the list of names on a war memorial? What other suggestions do you have for remembering things that are important?

The two Johns take up their positions at the front. John Two has a huge rocket-type firework sticking out of the back of his jacket and is carrying a bucket of stones. Both Johns should also be wearing poppies.

John One: Allow me to introduce myself. My name is John and this is my…

John Two: Friend.

John One: … associate… John. We represent the management.

John Two: Right! And today we are going to talk to you all about Christmas. Right, John?

John One: Wrong, John!

John Two: Sorry, John. I meant to say, 'Today we are going to talk to you about Easter.'

John One: Wrong again, John!

John Two: Harvest? … Lent? … EastEnders? … The Spice Girls? … Torchwood? … Bilbo Baggins?

Throughout this list, John One is shaking his head vehemently.

John One: John!

John Two: Sorry, John.

John One: We're here to talk about Remembrance Day.

John Two: Sorry, John. I forgot it was Remembrance Day.

John One: You… forgot… it was… Remembrance Day?! You've got a head like a sieve! What do you think that is, down the back of your jacket?

John Two suddenly sees the rocket and does an exaggerated 'double take'.

John Two: Oh! S'a rocket, innit?

John One: Yeah. And I'll give you a rocket in a minute if you don't pay attention!

John Two: But you already gave me this rocket, John. Before we came in.

John One: *(Gives him 'the look')* It's a visual aid, you dafty pot! It's supposed to remind you.

John Two: Ohhhh! Like 'Remember, remember, the fifth of November, gunpowder, cheese and some snot. I see no reason why gunpowder treason should ever be…' Erm, can't remember the rest, John.

John One: 'Forgot'! And it's treason and plot, not cheese and some snot. Anyway, the rocket is there to remind us of Bonfire night and the need to be really careful. Don't play with matches or stuff fireworks inside your clothes *(Looks meaningfully at John and the rocket)*.

John Two: Right, John! *(Suddenly remembers the rocket and pulls it out of his jacket.)*

John One: *(Taking the rocket from John Two)* But this also reminds us of the bombs and shells and bullets that cause so much death and destruction in war. We should never forget that. Never!

John Two: Right, John.

John One: Everyone should carry things that remind them of what's important. Like poppies.

John Two: Poppy's what? *(John One looks at him)* Oh, right. And what about these stones, John?

John One: In the rule book, the management often used stones to remind his people what was important.

John Two: Too right, John. Throw one of them at anybody, they wouldn't forget!

John One: They are definitely not for throwing, John! Any of you lot want to take a

Reproduced with permission from *More Collective Worship Unwrapped* published by BRF 2010 (978 1 84101 664 1) www.barnabasinschools.org.uk

stone on your way out, John here is going to leave this bucket by the door. Take a stone if you want to remember.

John Two: I'll have one of them, I think. I want to remember, but I keep forgetting to.

John One: You'd better take two stones, John.

John Two: Right, John.

The two Johns leave but stand by the door with the bucket on a chair, so that the children can take a small stone from it.

You could finish the assembly with some appropriate pictures of conflict displayed, some music and a time of reflection.

The Two Johns

Palm Sunday

STORYTELLING METHOD

Dramatic and humorous dialogue

Preparation

Take time to read through the script and allow for a short rehearsal. Also, allow time to prepare the costumes or to make contact with people to play the characters.

Bible link

Mark 11:1–11

Visual aids

❖ Two confident and imaginative actors dressed in DJs and shades
❖ A big Bible
❖ A PDA or similar palm device

> **Helpful hints:** Try to get your two Johns to stay 'in character' from the moment they enter the school hall to the moment they leave. They are supposed to appear intimidating and scary (in a humorous way). Most of the time, when they are not performing, they can just stand at the side and look menacing.

Main themes

Palm Sunday and Christ the King

Further topics covered
Authority and worship

Prayer

Dear Lord, thank you that you are king of all the earth. Help us to show respect for you and for all the earth, and to know when to shout your praises and when to be still. Thank you, Lord. Amen

Songs

Jesus, you are the king (KS)
Give me oil in my lamp (KS)
Who's the king of the jungle? (KS)

FOLLOW-UP

This sketch is an opportunity for the two Johns to chair a discussion on famous people—why they became famous and what we like (or dislike) about them. You could include film stars, sporting heroes, pop icons, historical figures and even fictional characters. This could lead on to a discussion of monarchy and what we like (or dislike) about it. Should we respect the Queen? How would we treat her if she came to visit? What is special about Jesus? Why did he enter Jerusalem on a donkey, a creature considered rather humorous, rather than on a great white horse, like a conquering hero? Is the idea of worship an outdated notion today? Do people still worship persons or things? Do we have a responsibility to worship God and, if so, why?

John One: Allow me to introduce myself. My name is John and this is my…

John Two: Friend.

John One: … associate… John. We represent the management.

John Two: Yeah. Right, John. 'Ere, John, I ain't half been looking forward to this, John. Celebrating technolology, John. Computers and all that. Mobile phones. Earpods.

John One: What are you talking about, John?

John Two: PALM Sunday, innit? I bought myself a Palm Pilot specially. *(He takes it out of his pocket and holds it up triumphantly.)* It's got everything. Fully integrated wossname, that thingy that makes beeping noises, windows, curtains and something called a soft office.

John One: John. Palm Sunday has nothing to do with Palm Pilots, mobile phones or any other technology. Palm Sunday is when Jesus came into Jerusalem on a donkey.

John Two: Well, I heard 'e was IT … I … T—you know, up to date with Information Technology, keeping him on the move and upwardly mobile.

John One: John, that's not even nearly funny. *(He takes the Palm from John Two and puts it in his pocket.)* Palm Sunday is the day the management has designated the beginning of Holy Week, leading up to Easter. Jesus wanted the people to realise he was important and special, so he came into town with a donkey instead of on a big white stallion.

John Two: I wouldn't have come in with a donkey or a stallion, John. If it was me, I'd have come in with a Jaguar. Cor, I'd love an E-type.

John One: Well, you ain't Jesus, John, and this was the way he did it! All the crowds realised he was somebody special when they saw him. They all waved palm branches off the trees and shouted, 'Hosanna! Hosanna!'

John Two: And did he know?

John One: Did he know what?

John Two: Who Anna was?

John One: HOSANNA. It's a special greeting for a king.

John Two: A king? I thought Jesus was a carpenter and a teacher.

John One: Yes, but he's a king as well, John. It says so in the rule book. The management has designated Jesus King of kings and Lord of lords.

John Two: Cor! Respect! Does that mean we have to call him Your Majesty, John?

John One: Too right, John. And what you lot have got to remember is that he's your king, too. He's the king of everything and everyone. And, like the crowds in Jerusalem on Palm Sunday, we should worship him too!

John Two: John?

John One: Yes, John?

John Two: Can I have my Palm Pilot back?

John One: Why, John?

John Two: I want to call all my mates and tell them the good news about King Jesus!

John One hands the Palm back to John Two, who 'dials' on it and starts talking as the two of them leave.

You could finish by displaying some pictures of the triumphal entry into Jerusalem, pictures of a recent royal event, or scenes of someone arriving at an airport or railway station to rapturous greeting, with some music and then a time of reflection.

Reproduced with permission from *More Collective Worship Unwrapped* published by BRF 2010 (978 1 84101 664 1) www.barnabasinschools.org.uk

The Two Johns

Mothering Sunday (Mothers' Day)

STORYTELLING METHOD

Dramatic and humorous dialogue

Preparation

Take time to read through the script and allow for a short rehearsal. Also, allow time to prepare the costumes or to make contact with people to play the characters.

Bible link

1 Samuel 2:18–21

Visual aids

❖ Two confident and imaginative actors dressed in DJs and shades
❖ A big Bible

Helpful hints: Try to get your two Johns to stay 'in character' from the moment they enter the school hall to the moment they leave. They are supposed to appear intimidating and scary (in a humorous way). Most of the time, when they are not performing, they can just stand at the side and look menacing.

Main themes

Mothering Sunday (Mother's Day)

Further topics covered
Love, care and gratitude

Prayer

Loving and caring God, thank you so much for our mums. Help us to show the same love, care and gratitude to them that they show to us. Please be close to all those who no longer see their mums and to those who wish to be mums but cannot. Thank you, Lord. Amen

Songs

Jesus, Jesus, here I am (KS)
From heaven you came (KS)
Thank you, Lord, for this fine day (JP)

FOLLOW-UP

This is a good chance for the Johns to lead a discussion on mothers and parenthood. There could be a quiz on famous mothers in history. What is your mum's favourite flower… colour… film… television programme… food… and so on? What is the most amazing thing your mum has ever done? What do you like most about your mum? What is the best thing you have ever done for your mum? What can we do to help those whose mums have died? When do you think it is most difficult to be a mum?

Maybe the children could paint, draw or even take a photograph of their mothers for display in a class art gallery. Plan to invite some mothers into school for a special event such as a class tea party or special assembly.

John One: Allow me to introduce myself. My name is John and this is my…

John Two: *(Silence)*

John One: … associate… John. We represent the management *(looking puzzled at John)*.

John Two: *(Silence)*

John One: Right, John? … Right… John?!

John Two: *(Putting his finger to his lips)* Mum's the word!

John One: Now what are you on about?

John Two: Mums! It's muvvers' day! Hah! Gotcha!

John One: You certainly got something, John. So what you getting your mother for Mothers' Day, then, John? Chocolates? Flowers? A nice card?

John Two: Nah! I promised I'd get the old girl some folding blinds. For the kitchen.

John One: Folding blinds, John? That's a bit odd, isn't it?

John Two: My dad said if we didn't get some blinds, it could be curtains for the whole family.

John One: Well, it would be curtains for a whole lot of people if it weren't for mothers, John.

John Two: Right, John.

John One: Think of all the things our mothers do for us. Wash us, dress us, feed us, care for us.

John Two: Yeah *(getting out a big spotted hanky to wipe his nose and eyes)*. Getting us out of bed in the morning. Cooking our breakfast. Doing our homework.

John One: You never told me your mum did your homework!

John Two: Oh! Er, no. Of course my mum didn't do my homework… my dad did that. But she done all them other things. Muvvers are great.

John One: Too right, John. We all need to remember to respect our parents and thank God for them. I hope you lot remember to thank your mums and do something really nice for them on Mothers' Day. The management says, 'Make your parents proud, especially your mother.'

John Two: Right, John. That's in the book of Proverbs, that is. Chapter 23.

John One: Absolutely right, John. How'd you know that?

John Two: My mum told me!

The two Johns leave.

You could show some pictures of mothers on a screen, followed by some reflection and prayer. Alternatively, you could do this at the beginning, before the two Johns come in.

Reproduced with permission from *More Collective Worship Unwrapped* published by BRF 2010 (978 1 84101 664 1) www.barnabasinschools.org.uk

The Two Johns

St George's Day

STORYTELLING METHOD

Dramatic and humorous dialogue

Preparation

Take time to read through the script and allow for a short rehearsal. Also, allow time to prepare the costumes or to make contact with people to play the characters.

Bible link

Revelation 12:7–12

Visual aids

❖ Two confident and imaginative actors dressed in DJs and shades.

> Helpful hints: Try to get your two Johns to stay 'in character' from the moment they enter the school hall to the moment they leave. They are supposed to appear intimidating and scary (in a humorous way). Most of the time, when they are not performing, they can just stand at the side and look menacing.

Main themes

St George's Day and character building

Further topics covered
The battle between good and evil

Prayer

Almighty God, you conquered sin and death once and for all on the cross. Please overcome the evil in our world with your all-powerful love. Amen

Songs

When a knight won his spurs (KS)
O when the saints (KS)
Jesus, we celebrate your victory (KS)

FOLLOW-UP

With the ongoing interest in fantasy literature, particularly the many movies associated with this genre, this might be a good opportunity for the Johns to chair a discussion on the age-old battle between good and evil. Be prepared to discuss *The Lord of the Rings*, *Harry Potter*, *The Chronicles of Narnia*, *His Dark Materials* and all the superheroes from DC and Marvel Comics that have made it to the silver screen. Don't forget to include the many excellent fantasy books that are being read, many of which will be in the school library. Why do you think there is such a fascination with the battle between good and evil? Does good always win? Spiderman was told, 'With great power comes great responsibility.' What does this mean and how should it affect us? If George never really killed a dragon and wasn't even English, why do you think he became our patron saint and is depicted so often fighting a dragon? Does the devil exist? Is there such a thing as absolute good and absolute evil? What is the difference between the battle between good and evil and the wars taking place on the earth today? How do you build a strong character and become someone who is 'brave and true'?

You could finish by inviting pictures of knights, warriors and dragons or even a short story competition on the subject of '[your name] and the Dragon'.

John One: Allow me to introduce myself. My name is John and this is my…

John Two: Friend.

John One: … associate… John. We represent the management.

John Two: Right, John!

John One: We're here today to talk to you about Saint George.

John Two: And the dragon, John, don't forget the dragon!

John One: George was probably born in Cappadocia, in modern-day Turkey, around AD270. His parents were Christians.

John Two: Never mind them, John. What about the dragon?

John One: George joined the Roman army and soon became famous for his bravery and good character.

John Two: And the dragon, John, don't forget the dragon!

John One: It was while he was in the Roman army that he spent some time in England, doing brave deeds…

John Two: Right, John! Like killing dragons!

John One: … and so, much later, being made the patron saint. *(Pause)*

John Two looks at him. John One smiles.

John Two: Is that it?

John One: Yup!

John Two: What about the flippin' dragon, John?

John One: Oh, that was just a legend, John.

John Two: No, no. He killed a great big gi-normous fire-breathing dragon. He did, John. I know he did. I saw it!

John One: Where, John?

John Two: In the movies.

John One: That was Eragon, John.

John Two: Was it?

John One: Yes, John.

John Two: So all that stuff about St George being a brave and true knight who killed a ferocious dragon what was menacing a fair maiden what was the king's only daughter is all a load of nonsense, then, is it, John?

John One: Well, no. Not completely, John. In the rule book, right at the end, the management tells us a little secret about the man downstairs.

John Two: Not… 'the man downstairs'?

John One: Right, John. And what God says is that the dragon is a picture of the man downstairs, who is sometimes called 'Satan' or 'the devil'.

John Two: Right, John.

John One: And the brave knight George, killing the evil dragon, is a picture of our victory over the devil.

John Two: So every time we stop something bad happening or stop the devil getting a hold on us and making us do something bad, it's like St George killing the dragon and rescuing the princess?

John One: You got it, John! *(Turning to the children)* And I hope you lot have got it an' all! Make George your patron saint and you could be like me and John here. Brave…

John Two: … and true!

They both salute and march off.

After the assembly it would be appropriate to show pictures of St George. You can find some at www.woodlands-junior.kent.sch.uk/customs/stgeorgepic.html along with some information gathered by Woodlands Junior School. This could be followed by some suitable music and a period of reflection.

Reproduced with permission from *More Collective Worship Unwrapped* published by BRF 2010 (978 1 84101 664 1) www.barnabasinschools.org.uk

Tree frogs and trainers

This assembly is entirely original because it is based upon a true event. I am grateful to Peter and to Stephan for allowing me to turn it into a story. Although this assembly is at the end of the KS2 section, it could probably be used for KS1 with some adaptation. I have put it at the end because it illustrates some key issues for schoolchildren—peer pressure and fashion. It also shows a vital life principle, which is about taking responsibility for our own happiness, coming up with a creative and imaginative idea and being determined enough to see it through.

STORYTELLING METHOD

Narrative

Preparation

Take time to read the story through and practise retelling it in your own words. You will also need to find a pair of top-of-the-range designer trainers.

Bible link

Esther 4:1-17

Visual aids

❖ A pair of top-of-the-range designer trainers
❖ Some pictures of designer labels

Helpful hints: This would be a good story to illustrate with line drawings on PowerPoint if you can find someone talented to draw them.

Main themes

Peer pressure and creative thinking

Further topics covered
Making a difference, designer labels and Fathers' Day

Prayer

Dear Father God, thank you for all dads. Help us to be determined and brave in all we do. Give us thoughtful ideas that will help to change the world. Thank you, Lord. Amen

Songs

I'm inright, outright, upright, downright (KS)
I want to be a tree that's bearing fruit (KS)
Shine, Jesus, shine (KS)

FOLLOW-UP

This is a good chance to discuss peer pressure and designer labels as well as enterprise and creative ideas. Has anyone ever been in a situation like Stephan's? How did you handle it? Why are labels so important? How does it feel to be different from others in your class? How important are style, fashion and image? Have you ever had a good idea? What did you do about it? What would you like to do when you leave school? How hard is it to finish a project that takes a long time? What lessons do you think Stephan and his dad learned about tree frogs and trainers?

Once upon a time, there was a father and there was a son. The son's name was Stephan. Like most fathers and sons, Stephan and his dad loved each other very much. So when Stephan's dad promised to take him shopping in town one weekend, the boy was very excited. He had seen a pair of designer-label trainers in the local department store and they were so-o-o-o cool! They were top of the range and just like the ones his mate John wore to school every day. Stephan's old trainers were faded and scuffed and he pictured himself turning up to school on Monday morning in these beauties. Neat! To Stephan's great delight, his dad had seen that he needed a new pair of trainers and even suggested they go out together and buy them. Then maybe afterwards they'd go and see a new film at the cinema.

Stephan got up that Saturday morning feeling very excited. He gobbled down his breakfast and pulled on his favourite hoodie. Dad was waiting in the car and before long they were walking down the aisle of the shoe department in the nearby town.

'Got any special trainers in mind, Stephan?' said his dad.

'Well, Dad,' said Stephan with a big grin. 'It's funny you should say that...' He pointed over at the shiny white-and-blue designer trainers on the shelf nearby. Dad made a rueful face. 'I don't think so, Stephan. There's no way I am paying out that much money for a pair of training shoes! What about this pair on the shelf below? They look identical and they're less than half the price of the other ones.'

Dad's voice kind of faded in and out of Stephan's mind and he suddenly felt like his head would explode. It had never crossed his mind that Dad wouldn't buy the trainers! He looked at Dad again, hardly hearing what was being said. Dad had actually got the other pair of shoes off the shelf and was holding them out to Stephan.

'But I don't want those!' said Stephan, much louder than he intended. 'Nobody wears those rubbish shoes nowadays. All my class have cool designer trainers. I want some, too!'

'Get used to disappointment, Stephan,' said his dad resolutely, 'because there is no way under the sun I am buying them for you.'

Stephan's face fell and, suddenly, he hated his dad. Everybody else's dad got their sons the designer trainers they wanted. Everybody else's dads listened to their sons. Why, he'd even told John he was getting some new designer-label trainers. All his mates in school would be laughing at him and it was all his dad's fault. He turned round and stormed out of the shop.

His dad went after him, of course, and they had a big row in the car park. They shouted at each other, and they both said things that maybe they shouldn't, and they went home without seeing the film. For the whole weekend Stephan stayed in his room and wouldn't speak to his dad.

Stephan dreaded going to school on Monday. He'd ended up with no new trainers at all so he still had to wear his old ones. He explained to John before class that he was still getting some new ones but his parents had been too busy to get them this weekend. It was a miserable day for Stephan. Double maths and a whole day of looking at rubbish trainers!

On his way home, Stephan passed the pet shop on the corner of Montague Street. He liked looking at the rabbits and gerbils in the window, and sometimes there was a litter of puppies or some kittens. Mr Nawaz, the owner, had got a tank full of tree frogs some days back and Stephan had been fascinated by their bright colours and glistening bodies. As he pressed his nose mournfully up against the glass and watched the frogs enjoying their meal of grasshoppers, he suddenly had an idea. He rushed into the shop to speak to Mr Nawaz.

Later that night, just before it got dark, Dad was amazed to see Stephan in the field behind their house, rushing around with the old butterfly net from the cellar.

'Stephan!' called Dad as he went out through the garden gate. 'It's nearly supper time. What on earth are you doing?'

Stephan looked slightly embarrassed as his dad

came over to him. Dad saw that he had a large cardboard box with some holes punched in it on the grass beside him.

'Oh hi, Dad,' said Stephan. 'I'm catching grasshoppers. Look!' Dad saw that there were nearly a dozen in the box already. 'What's this, Stephan?' asked Dad. 'A science project for school?'

'No, Dad,' explained Stephan. 'They're for Mr Nawaz' tree frogs. Mr Nawaz—you know he owns the pet shop in town—can't get hold of fresh grasshoppers very easily. He says the frogs really only like the ones that are alive and jumping about. So I'm catching some fresh ones for him.'

'Well, that's very commendable, Stephan,' replied his dad, 'but I really think…'

'I'm selling them to him,' beamed Stephan. 'Five for 1p.' Stephan gulped and looked down. 'I really do want those trainers, Dad.'

Stephan's dad smiled. 'Well, you'll need to catch hundreds and thousands of grasshoppers to raise enough to buy the trainers, and that's not easy. I hope you know what you've let yourself in for.' Dad picked up the box and father and son went in for supper together.

Every night after he'd done his homework, Stephan went out into the field. For half an hour he rushed around catching grasshoppers, and every morning before school he took the grasshoppers to Mr Nawaz' pet shop for the tree frogs. Dad came home on Tuesday evening with the designer-label trainers, but at the end of the week he held out his hand for the first instalment from Stephan.

It took Stephan 14 and a half weeks to pay Dad back for the new trainers, and catching so many grasshoppers took a lot of skill and patience. When he dropped the final pile of coins into Dad's hands, Stephan heaved a huge sigh of relief.

'You know, I'm really proud of you, Stephan,' said his father. 'That was a very enterprising idea and a brave decision. So I've got a little surprise for you. You see, I didn't pay all your 10 and 20 and 50 pences into the bank. I kept them!' And with a big warm fatherly smile he reached under his desk and pulled out a large cardboard box with all the grasshopper coins inside. 'Well,' he said, 'you never know when you might need another pair of trainers!'

I'm not sure whether I can say they both lived happily ever after, but I can say that, for some time, there was a happy father, a happy son and lots of happy tree frogs!

Reproduced with permission from *More Collective Worship Unwrapped* published by BRF 2010 (978 1 84101 664 1) **www.barnabasinschools.org.uk**

Photocopiable visuals

The following visuals are also available for download free of charge from the website, www.barnabasinschools.org.uk/morecollectiveworship.

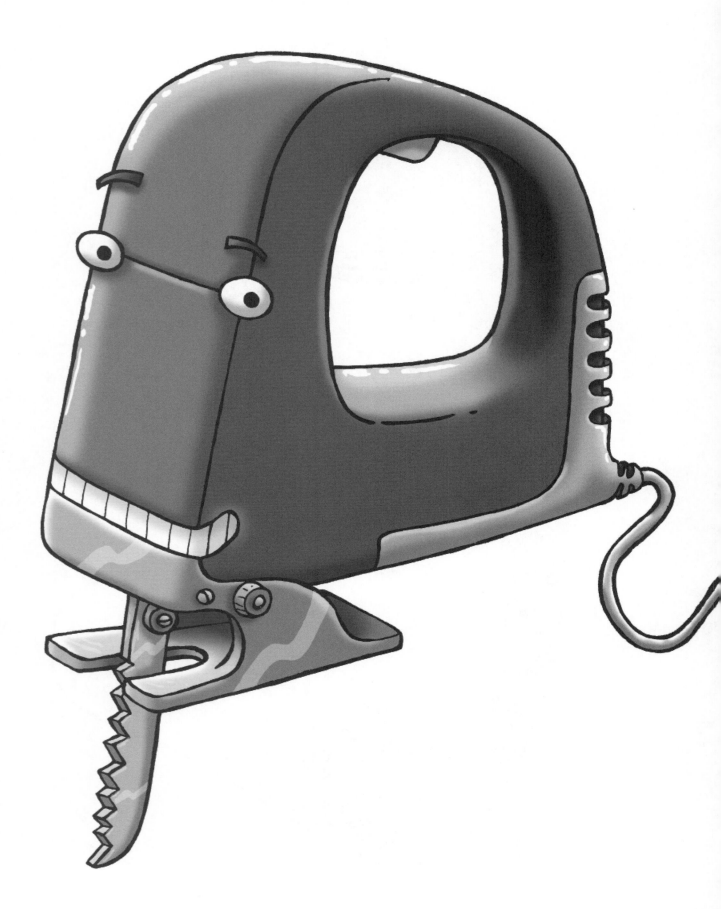

Billy the Big Hammer

Sally the Small Hammer

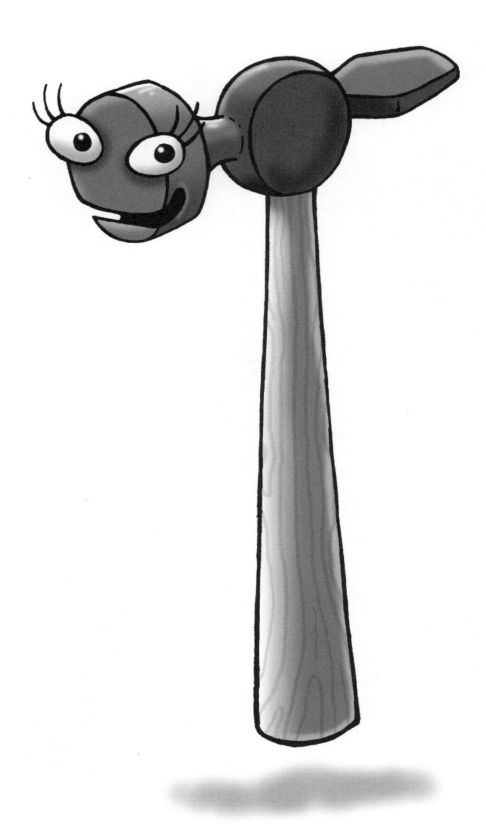

Clara the Chisel

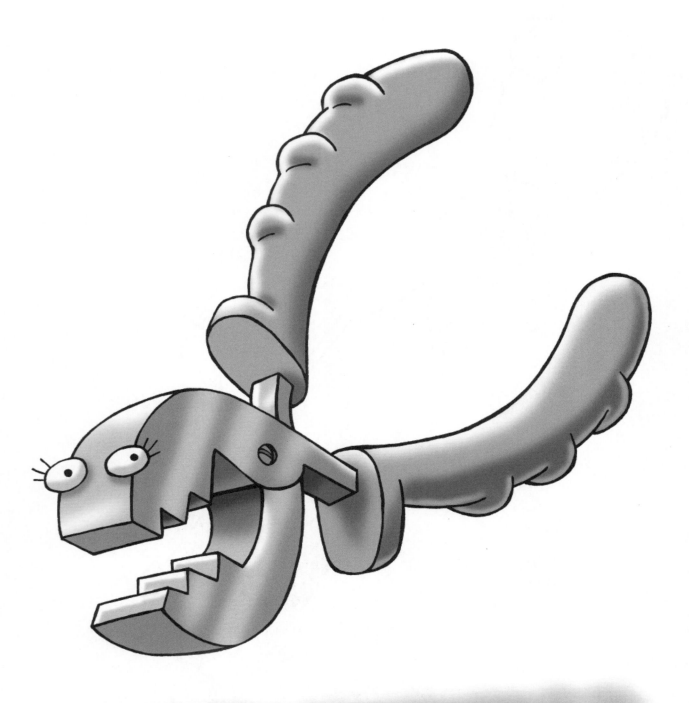

Sammy the Screwdriver

Timmy the Tilecutter

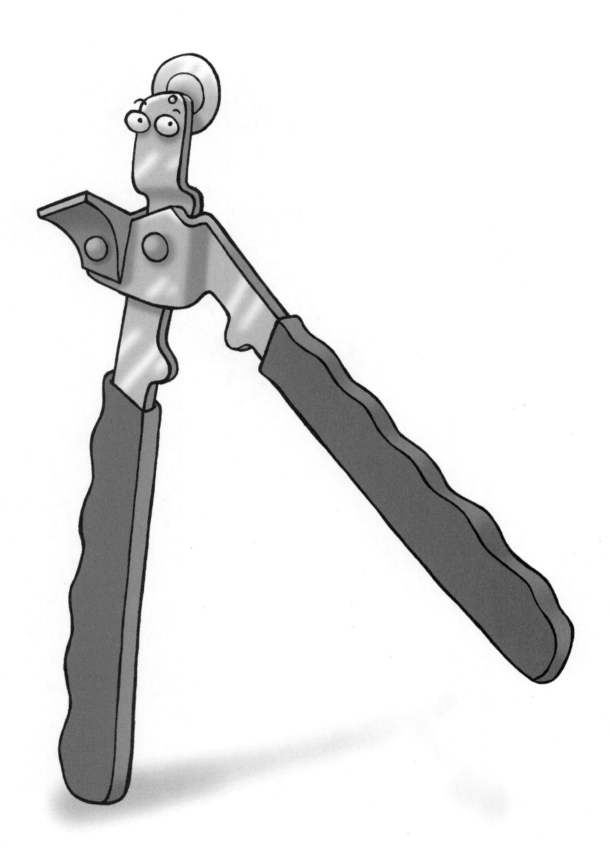

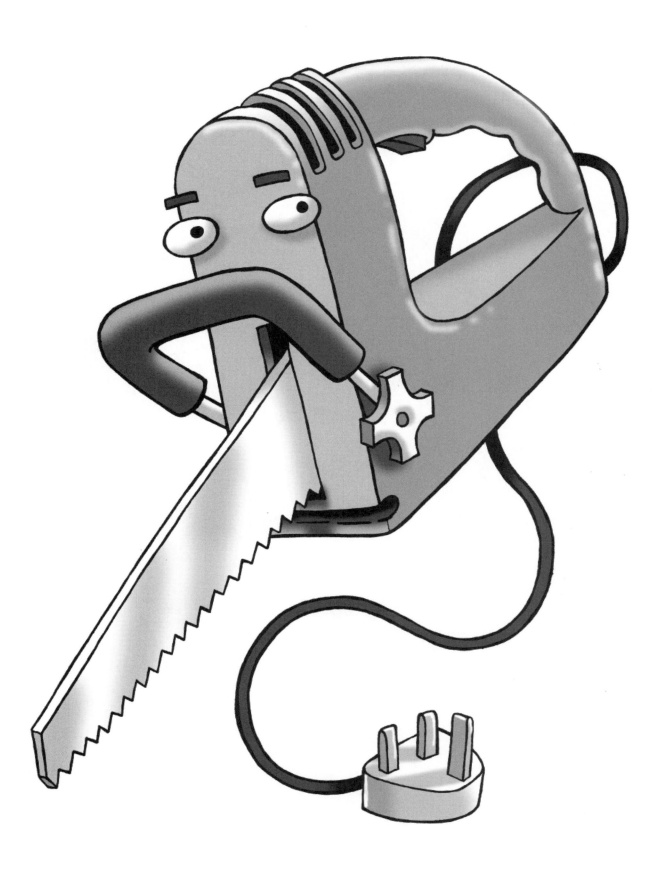

Reproduced with permission from *More Collective Worship Unwrapped* published by BRF 2010 (978 1 84101 664 1) www.barnabasinschools.org.uk

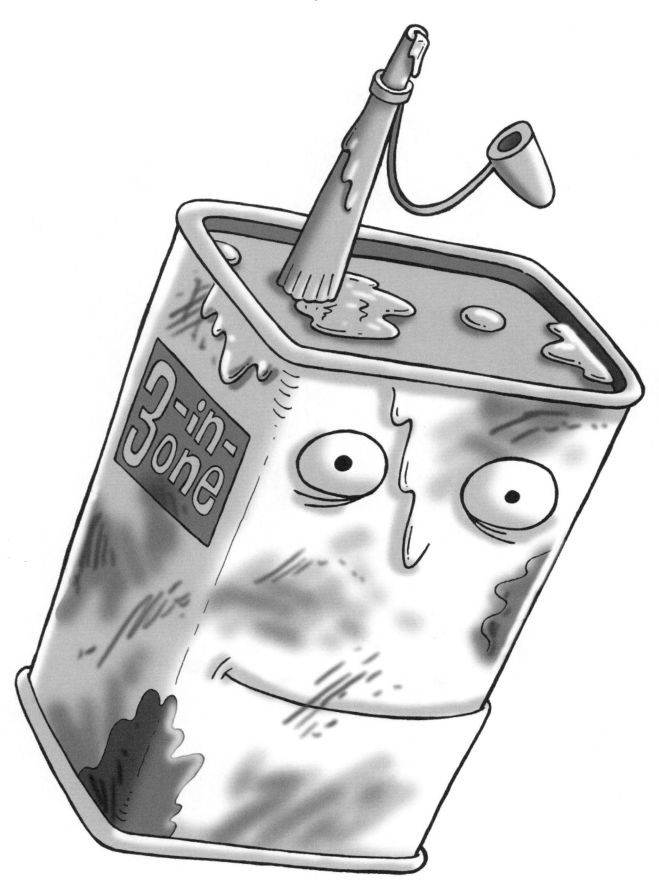

Honky the Donkey

Index of themes

Index of Bible links

Resources

www.barnabasinschools.org.uk
One of the best websites you will find on working with primary schools. A veritable cornucopia of ideas including RE days for primary schools and INSET days for staff; lots of excellent books including mine.

www.bible.com
Zondervan's site for all matters connected to the Bible. Includes many versions and languages.

www.bible.org.uk
The website for *Bible Explorer* and *Walk Through the Bible*.

www.biblegateway.com
Another excellent resource for anyone who wishes to access many versions of the Bible, commentaries and notes.

www.brf.org.uk
The website for the Bible Reading Fellowship (my publishers and a wonderful bunch of people!).

www.cesew.org.uk
The website of the Catholic Education Service, with much information on RC schools.

www.christianeducation.org.uk
Information on Collective Worship and RE.

www.christian-teachers.org.uk
The website for the Association of Christian Teachers (ACT).

www.churcharmy.org.uk
The evangelism wing of the Church of England. Also involved in working with schools.

www.churches-together.net
Churches Together in England website. Some good links for schools. They published an excellent booklet called *Linking Churches and Schools* (see details on p. 100).

www.classroom-assistant.net
Useful information about being a classroom assistant.

www.cofe.anglican.org
The Church of England's official website (and very good it is, too!). Useful links to church schools.

www.crb.gov.uk
Everything you need to know about the Criminal Records Bureau and CRB checks.

www.culham.ac.uk
Lots of helpful links to RE and Collective Worship.

www.curbsproject.org.uk
Website of the CURBS (Children in Urban Situations) project. Believing that all children are created in God's image, CURBS starts in the world of the urban child and, through positive relationships, seeks to build bridges which will enable children who live in urban areas to experience God's loving care.

www.dfes.gov.uk
Government education site.

www.educationsunday.org
Churches Together in England site with information for Education Sunday.

www.everychildmatters.gov.uk
Everything you wanted to know about the Every Child Matters agenda.

www.faithworks.info
Faithworks exists to resource, inspire and speak up for the needs of local communities and positively influence society as a whole.

www.gloucestershire.gov.uk
A good example of the work being done by SACRE in one particular LEA.

www.governornet.co.uk
Everything you wanted to know about being a school governor.

http://curriculum.qca.org.uk
All matters associated with the National Curriculum.

www.openthebook.net
As the site itself says: 'enabling every child to hear the story of the Bible at school in their primary years'. A great website!

www.pace-trust.org.uk
The website for PACE (Programme for Applied Christian Education), a superb group based in Poole and supporting a number of pastoral workers in local schools.

www.portage.org.uk
The website for the National Portage Association of Britain.

www.qca.org.uk
The Qualifications and Curriculum Authority. Many good links, including to SACRE.

www.learningwithsouthglos.org
Another good example of the work being done by SACRE in one particular LEA. There is also some useful advice on protocols when visiting other places of worship.

www.kingston.gov.uk/religious_believers_visiting_schools-3.pdf
Download the PCfRE booklet *Religious Believers Visiting Schools* here.

www.scriptureunion.org.uk
Probably the largest Christian organisation in the country placing workers into schools. Well worth visiting their website.

www.sgoss.org.uk/home
The website for the school governors' 'one-stop shop'.

www.spinnaker.org.uk
The website of the Spinnaker Trust, with resources for assemblies.

www.standards.dfes.gov.uk
The Standards Site for the Department of Children and Families.

www.surestart.gov.uk
Everything you wanted to know about Sure Start.

www.teachingexpertise.com
The website for Optimus Education. Lots of resources.

www.teachre.com
Promotes Religious Education.

www.theredirectory.org.uk
A multifaith site for Religious Education.

www.reonline.org.uk
Resources for RE and Collective Worship.

www.veritas.ie
Lots of online books and resources. Source for James Norman's book, *At the Heart of Education: School Chaplaincy and Pastoral Care*.

USEFUL ASSEMBLY BOOKS

77 Talks for 21st-Century Kids, Chris Chesterton (Monarch, 2008, ISBN 978 0 82546 019 7)

Assemblies Across Faiths, Gerald Haigh and Jane West (Optimus, 2007, ISBN 978 1 90553 832 4)

Assemblies for Autumn Festivals, Martin Cox (Barnabas, 2007, ISBN 978 1 84101 459 3)

Bible Storybags, Margaret Cooling (Barnabas, 2008, ISBN 978 1 84101 532 3)

Collective Worship Unwrapped, John Guest (Barnabas, 2005, ISBN 978 1 84101 371 8)

Eyewitness Assemblies, Gaynor Cobb (Barnabas, 2007, ISBN 978 1 84101 496 8)

Stories for Interactive Assemblies, Nigel Bishop (Barnabas, 2006, ISBN 978 1 84101 465 4)

The Almost Instant Assembly Book, Sue and Chris Govus (Kevin Mayhew, 1999, ISBN 978 1 84003 373 1)

The Gospels Unplugged, Lucy Moore (Barnabas, 2002, ISBN 978 1 84101 243 8)

The Lord's Prayer Unplugged, Lucy Moore (Barnabas, 2004, ISBN 978 1 84101 262 9)

Through the Year with Timothy Bear, Brian Sears (Barnabas, 2006, ISBN 978 1 84101 394 7)

Ugly Bugs and Apple Trees, Michael Catchpool and Pat Lunt (Kevin Mayhew, 2002, ISBN 978 1 84003 899 6)

Wisdom for Worship, Margaret Cooling (Stapleford, 1995, ISBN 978 0 95165 373 9) (out of print)

BEREAVEMENT RESOURCE BOOKS

Badger's Parting Gifts, Susan Varley (Collins Picture Lions, 1994, ISBN 978 0 00664 317 3)

Love You Forever, Robert Munsch (Firefly Books, 1986, ISBN 978 0 92066 837 5)

Someone Special Has Died (St Christopher's Hospice, 1989) (see www.stchristophers.org.uk)

Where Did Grandad Go?, Catherine House (Barnabas, 2006, ISBN 978 1 84101 502 6)

MORE USEFUL RESOURCE BOOKS

35 Stories to Make You Think, Heather Butler (Barnabas, 2008, ISBN 978 1 84101 506 4)

God Is Always With Me, Helen Caswell (Lutterworth, 1989, ISBN 978 0 71882 796 0)

Linking Churches and Schools, Gillian Wood (Churches Together in England, 2003, ISBN 978 1 87429 523 5) (out of print)

Mission-Shaped Children, Margaret Withers (CHP, 2006, ISBN 978 0 71514 081 9)

Reflective Learning, Trevor Reader and Lilian Weatherley (Barnabas, 2009, ISBN 978 1 84101 573 6)

Storytelling: A Practical Guide, Lance Pierson (SU, 1997, ISBN 978 1 85999 094 0) (out of print)

Tales of Grace, Eve Lockett (Barnabas, 2005, ISBN 978 1 84101 366 4)

The Adventures of Naughty Nora, Stephen Cottrell (Barnabas, 2008, ISBN 978 1 84101 388 6)

The Barnabas Schools' Bible, Rhona Davies (Barnabas, 2007, ISBN 978 1 84101 564 4)

You Are Special, Max Lucado (Candle Books, 2005, ISBN 978 1 85985 590 4)

SONG BOOKS FOR COLLECTIVE WORSHIP

Alleluya! 77 Songs for Thinking People, eds. David Gadsby and John Hoggarth (A&C Black, 1980, ISBN 978 0 71361 997 3)

Brown Bread and Butter, ed. Alison McMorland (Ward Lock Educational, 1982, ISBN 978 0 70624 196 9)

Children's Sunnyday Songbook, ed. Peter Foss (International Music Publications, 2005, ISBN 978 0 86359 467 0)

Come and Praise Books 1 & 2, ed. Geoffrey Marshall-Taylor, arr. Douglas Coombes (BBC Educational, 1988, ISBN 978 0 56334 249 6)

Come and Sing Some More, ed. Ann Broad (SU, 1982, ISBN 978 0 85421 948 3)

MISCELLANEOUS

Up, Up and Away (modelling balloon suppliers): Unit 17, Newlands End, Laindon North Industrial Estate, Laindon, Basildon, Essex SS15 6DU
Tel: 01268 411712; Fax: 01268 541171

Unit 1, Wellington Park Estate, Waterloo Road, Staples Corner, London NW2 7UA
Tel: 0208 8452 9700; Fax: 0208452 6900

www.upupandaway.co.uk

(This supplier is 'trade only' so you would need to register as a 'trader'.)

Collective Worship Unwrapped

33 tried and tested story-based assemblies for primary schools

Collective worship provides an important opportunity at the beginning of the school day to address the 'awe and wonder' part of learning. With this in mind, this book offers tried and tested primary assemblies with a Christian focus for Key Stages One and Two. Each assembly is complete and ready to run, with memorable stories, Bible links written in full, ideas for visual aids, helpful hints, prayers, suggested songs and follow-up material.

The assemblies cover a host of themes, some topical, some on moral and personal development, citizenship or spiritual values, and some linking in to seasons of the Christian year.

Many of the stories use a specific storytelling technique (such as telling a story from an unusual angle, using a 'tagline', repetition and audience participation), making this a flexible and practical resource, ideal for newly qualified teachers seeking to grasp the key principles of collective worship as quickly and as effectively as possible—but equally valuable for experienced teachers, RE coordinators and those invited into schools to lead collective worship.

Includes photocopy permission.

Available direct from BRF using the order form on page 111 or online at www.barnabasinschools.org.uk.

Stories for Interactive Assemblies

15 story-based assemblies to get children talking

Nigel Bishop

Collective worship is an ideal time to combine biblical teaching with contemporary storytelling. The 15 easy-to-tell, contemporary stories in this book are all based in the world of the classroom but have their roots in the parables of Jesus. They are designed to stimulate children's thinking and get them talking in the assembly and afterwards in the classroom.

As a means of teaching, the parables are vivid, challenging and memorable. They have been described as 'earthly stories with a heavenly meaning'. Primary children of all ages will recognise themselves and their classmates in the stories and, even if they do not recognise the original story, they are invited to relate to the underlying message that is the essence of the parable.

Each story is followed by questions for the assembly or classroom, designed to help the children interact with some of the issues raised, plus suggestions for practical activities, based on different learning styles.

Each story also includes:

- A target theme to help direct the teacher towards the main teaching objective.
- A prayer or reflection to close the assembly if desired.
- Bible references for the original parables.
- Information to link the teaching to PSHE/Citizenship and the non-statutory national framework for RE or local SACRE guidelines.

Available direct from BRF using the order form on page 111 or online at www.barnabasinschools.org.uk.

Eyewitness Assemblies

15 ready-to-use assemblies for Easter to Pentecost

Gaynor Cobb

From Palm Sunday to Pentecost, *Eyewitness Assemblies* presents 15 short stories giving imaginative 'first hand' accounts told from the perspective of a character in the original Bible story. The eyewitness account is followed by a reflective poem, role-play or news report to help spark children's imagination and enable them to get under the skin of the story. Each unit is stand-alone, while at the same time giving a clear and comprehensive picture of the part of the Christian story that led to Jesus' death and resurrection and the birth of the early Church.

Each unit comprises:

- Background information
- Bible references with key verses written in full
- Ideas for using the material
- Discussion starters
- Focused links into PSHE/Citizenship and RE
- Ideas for visual demonstrations
- Eyewitness story
- Follow-up questions
- Reflective poem or news report
- Suggestions for prayer, songs and music

The material is ideal for Key Stage 2, and class or whole-school assemblies, over the Easter period or in RE at other times of year.

Overall notes give general PSHE/Citizenship and RE links so that the assemblies could be followed up in class. This may be of particular use where the assembly forms part of the RE syllabus. There is also a helpful glossary and Bible index.

Available direct from BRF using the order form on page 111 or online at www.barnabasinschools.org.uk.

Assemblies for Autumn Festivals

27 ready-to-use ideas for festivals and feast days

Martin Cox

This book is packed with 27 tried and tested assembly ideas designed to resource both popular and lesser-known festivals in the first term of the new school year. The ideas fall under four main themes—Harvest, Saints, Remembrance and Advent—with at least two assemblies to choose from within each theme.

The material is flexible in that the assemblies can be used with a 'dip in and try' approach, followed in date order, or used to explore one of the four key themes. Topics covered include Harvest, St Matthew, Michaelmas, St Francis, St Luke, All Saints, Guy Fawkes, Remembrance, Christ the King, St Andrew, St Nicholas and Advent.

Each assembly includes key background information for the teacher, Bible links, creative ideas for introducing the theme, suggestions for visual aids and ideas for exploring the theme, including storytelling, drama, music, songs and prayers. Also, each assembly is backed up by a wealth of ideas for cross-curricular extension work in the classroom.

Available direct from BRF using the order form on page 111 or online at www.barnabasinschools.org.uk.

Through the Year with Timothy Bear

24 five-minute stories for special days and seasons of the year

Brian Sears

Meet Timothy Bear, who, together with his family and friends, finds himself at the centre of many adventures guaranteed to appeal to young children. The 24 stories in this book are ideal for use in collective worship and assemblies, PSHE and circle time, as an aid to the teaching of RE or purely for enjoyment at story time.

There is a story for all major special days throughout the year, as well as stories for each of the four seasons, making the material an ideal resource to teach biblical and moral truths to 5–7s throughout the year. Each story includes a seasonal theme, PSHE links and Bible links, including the key passage in full. There is also follow-up material for the assembly or classroom, offering ways to help young children to:

- get to grips with the story.
- express the story.
- own the story.
- live out the story.

Available direct from BRF using the order form on page 111 or online at www.barnabasinschools.org.uk.

35 Stories to Make You Think

Teaching values through RE

Heather Butler

35 Stories to Make You Think is a new and revised compilation of the popular *Stories to Make You Think* series, addressing a range of topical and often sensitive issues relevant to the lives of children in Years 3–6. It can be used on a one-to-one basis, in a group or with a whole class during circle time, PSHE, Citizenship or RE. The 35 issues are covered under four distinct headings: Family life, Life and death, Community life and Personal life.

Each chapter follows the same format and includes:

- Story summary
- RE concept
- Exploring the concept
- Key Bible verse
- Bible story link
- Story time
- Things children have said
- Thinking time for children
- Thinking time activity
- Optional prayer

Available direct from BRF using the order form on page 111 or online at www.barnabasinschools.org.uk.

Reflective Learning

Unpacking key Christian beliefs in RE and collective worship

Trevor Reader and Lilian Weatherley

Reflective Learning provides teachers with essential background information for key Christian beliefs and offers important tools to instil confidence in the teaching of RE. The material focuses on three key concepts related to the principal beliefs of the Christian faith as follows:

- Who God is (the Trinity): Three units comprising the stories of creation, re-creation and baptism.
- What God has done (Salvation): Five units comprising the stories of Christmas and Epiphany, Lent, Holy Week, Easter and Pentecost.
- The Church today (Reflective living): Three units relating to the journey of life—belonging and believing, sharing and caring, and patterns for living.

Each unit starts with an in-depth classroom-based exploration of the concept, with background information for the teacher, ideas for exploring the story, questions about the story, introductory tasks, key symbols, and ideas for understanding the story through the five senses. The classroom material for each unit is supported by two comprehensive outlines for acts of collective worship for assembly, each of which follows a common format, including ideas for applying the material and suggestions for songs and prayer.

Alongside the class work and assembly material, creative ideas are given for setting up a theme-based focus table for the classroom.

Available direct from BRF using the order form on page 111 or online at www.barnabasinschools.org.uk.

The Adventures of Naughty Nora

14 fun stories of everyday life for collective worship, assemblies and storytelling in the classroom

Stephen Cottrell

Naughty Nora is the naughtiest girl in her school. There is a little bit of naughtiness inside everybody, but just imagine taking all those little bits of naughtiness and putting them inside one person! Well, that gives you some idea of how naughty Naughty Nora is. She is *very* naughty indeed.

But, like many naughty people, as well as getting into trouble, Naughty Nora knows how to say 'sorry'. She knows about fun, forgiveness, mischief, joy and grace. This book is the story of her adventures.

The intention of the stories is that (in a similar way to the parables we find in the Bible) they will encourage children to think through the ideas and make connections to their own experiences of school, home and the teachings of the Christian faith.

At the end of each story there are questions to promote discussion, sayings of Jesus with Bible references, a prayer, and hints on retelling the story. Each element is designed to help the storyteller lead children into a deeper understanding of the story and to question and explore it.

The stories are ideal for:

- Collective worship
- Class assemblies
- RE and storytelling in the classroom
- Independent reading

Available direct from BRF using the order form on page 111 or online at www.barnabasinschools.org.uk.

Tales of Grace

50 five-minute stories for all-age talks, sermons and assemblies

Eve Lockett

'Stories help us to see from different angles, they free us to explore our own feelings and beliefs, they engage our emotions as well as our minds, they speak to adults and children alike and they connect us with each other.'

This book contains a wealth of imaginative five-minute stories written with both children and adults in mind. They can be used with only children present, only adults present, or with a mixed-age group and are suitable for use in:

- Church services
- Children's talks
- Family services
- Sunday clubs
- School assemblies
- After-school clubs
- Bedtime or family reading
- Group reflection

The stories illustrate some of the main themes of the Christian life, such as grace, forgiveness, friendship, guidance, trust and prayer. Some have a traditional flavour, others a contemporary setting. Each story is accompanied by sermon pointers for four key Bible passages relating to the theme, questions for young listeners and suggestions for visual aids and actions.

Available direct from BRF using the order form on page 111 or online at www.barnabasinschools.org.uk.

The Barnabas Schools' Bible

Rhona Davies

This new Children's Bible includes stories chosen to cover all the main events, retold with a continuous thread.

There are 365 stories, one for every day of the year, each accompanied by Bible quotations from a real Bible translation, giving readers a taste of the language and style of the original texts.

The stylish illustrations (by Marcin Piwowarski) illuminate and inform, while the easily accessible encyclopedia at the end of the book helps to explain the context and background of the stories. All combine to make this a useful and readable Bible for older children.

Available direct from BRF using the order form on page 111 or online at www.barnabasinschools.org.uk.

ORDER FORM

REF	TITLE	PRICE	QTY	TOTAL
371 8	Collective Worship Unwrapped	£12.99		
465 4	Stories for Interactive Assemblies	£6.99		
496 8	Eyewitness Assemblies	£7.99		
459 3	Assemblies for Autumn Festivals	£7.99		
394 7	Through the Year with Timothy Bear	£7.99		
506 4	35 Stories to Make You Think	£9.99		
573 6	Reflective Learning	£8.99		
388 6	The Adventures of Naughty Nora	£6.99		
366 4	Tales of Grace	£7.99		
564 4	The Barnabas Schools' Bible	£12.99		
		Postage and packing		
		Donation		
		TOTAL		

POSTAGE AND PACKING CHARGES

Order value	UK	Europe	Surface	Air Mail
£7.00 & under	£1.25	£3.00	£3.50	£5.50
£7.10–£30.00	£2.25	£5.50	£6.50	£10.00
Over £30.00	FREE	prices on request		

Name _____ Account Number _____

Address _____

_____ Postcode _____

Telephone Number_____

Email _____

Payment by: ❑ Cheque ❑ Mastercard ❑ Visa ❑ Postal Order ❑ Maestro

Card no ☐☐☐☐ ☐☐☐☐ ☐☐☐☐ ☐☐☐☐ ☐☐☐

Valid from ☐☐☐ Expires ☐☐☐ Issue no. ☐☐☐

Security code* ☐☐☐ *Last 3 digits on the reverse of the card.
ESSENTIAL IN ORDER TO PROCESS YOUR ORDER

Shaded boxes for Maestro use only

Signature _____ Date _____

All orders must be accompanied by the appropriate payment.

Please send your completed order form to:
BRF, 15 The Chambers, Vineyard, Abingdon OX14 3FE
Tel. 01865 319700 / Fax. 01865 319701 Email: enquiries@brf.org.uk

❑ Please send me further information about BRF publications.

Available from your local Christian bookshop.   BRF is a Registered Charity

Resourcing **Collective Worship and Assemblies, RE, Festivals, Drama** and **Art** in primary schools

- Barnabas RE Days—exploring Christianity creatively
- INSET
- Books and resources
- www.barnabasinschools.org.uk

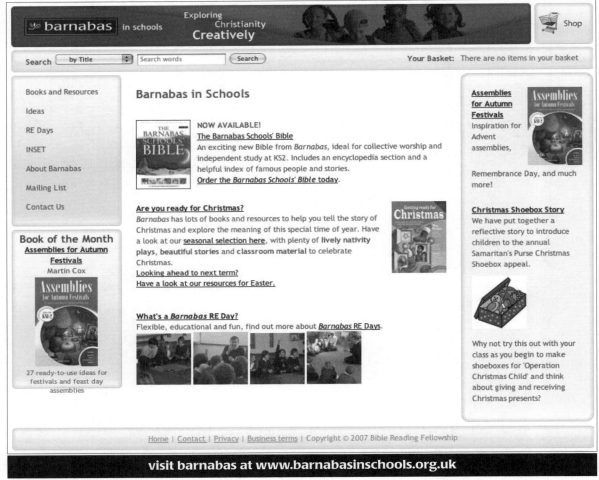

Have you signed up to receive the Barnabas monthly email?

To receive mailings about *Barnabas* resources and services, sign up at:

www.barnabasinschools.org.uk